tapas

100 everyday recipes

This edition published by Parragon Books Ltd in 2013
LOVE FOOD is an imprint of Parragon Books Ltd

Parragon Books Ltd
Chartist House
15–17 Trim Street
Bath BA1 1HA, UK
www.parragon.com/lovefood

ISBN 978-1-4723-4629-2

Printed in China

Produced by Ivy Contract
Cover photography by Mike Cooper
Cover image home economy and food styling by Lincoln Jefferson

Notes for the Reader

This book uses both metric and imperial measurements. Follow the same units of measurement throughout; do not mix metric and imperial. All spoon measurements are level: teaspoons are assumed to be 5 ml, and tablespoons are assumed to be 15 ml. Unless otherwise stated, milk is assumed to be full fat, eggs and individual vegetables are medium, and pepper is freshly ground black pepper. Unless otherwise stated, all root vegetables should be peeled prior to using.

Garnishes, decorations and serving suggestions are all optional and not necessarily included in the recipe ingredients or method. The times given are an approximate guide only. Preparation times differ according to the techniques used by different people and the cooking times may also vary from those given. Optional ingredients, variations or serving suggestions have not been included in the time calculations.

tapas

introduction

Tapas has become very popular and a bit of a buzzword in the last few years, but what exactly is tapas, and where does the idea come from?

Tapas is the collective name for small, delicious mouthfuls of something savoury, served with a chilled white wine, beer or sherry. It comes from tapa, the Spanish word for lid – specifically, the 'lid' created by the slice of bread that an innkeeper would thoughtfully place on top of a customer's wine glass to keep out the flies and dust between sips. The Andalucians then came up with the idea of balancing a morsel of something tasty on top of the bread to nibble on – a few slices of cheese or ham – and a new Spanish institution was born. Today, tapas are served in almost every bar throughout Spain. Usually they are displayed on the bar, and the waiter puts your selection on a plate, for eating either standing up or seated at the bar or a table.

Everything about tapas, from the preparation to eating and enjoying it, is a uniquely Spanish experience. Tapas are what eating with family and friends is all about, a true feast for the senses – they look and smell delectable and taste even better. Serve them on pretty plates in bright colours to bring a little Spanish sunshine to a cloudy day.

How you use tapas is up to you. A simple selection of these bite-size gastronomic glories can be served with drinks before lunch or dinner, or an array of dishes can make an informal lunch or dinner in themselves. Tapas are made from a wonderful variety of foods – meat, seafood, eggs, nuts and cheese, as well as every vibrant vegetable imaginable, in healthy Mediterranean style, with dips and sauces to add yet more flavour and interest to the tapas experience.

Eating tapas goes hand-in-hand with hospitality, friendship and plenty of good conversation, so tuck in, forget the cares of the day and linger, Spanish-style, with your favourite people.

nibbles

deep-fried green chillies

ingredients

serves 4–6

olive oil, for frying
250 g/9 oz sweet or hot
     fresh green chillies
sea salt

method

1 Heat 7.5 cm/3 inches of olive oil in a large, heavy-based saucepan until it reaches 180–190°C/350–375°F, or until a cube of bread turns brown in 30 seconds.

2 Rinse the chillies and pat them very dry with kitchen paper. Drop them in the hot oil for no longer than 20 seconds, or until they turn bright green and the skins blister.

3 Remove with a slotted spoon and drain well on crumpled kitchen paper. Sprinkle with sea salt and serve immediately.

tomato bread

ingredients

serves 4

4 slices French bread
2 ripe tomatoes, halved
1 garlic clove, finely chopped
    (optional)
2 tbsp olive oil (optional)

method.

1 Preheat the grill. Toast the bread under a hot grill until lightly golden on both sides.

2 Rub each slice of bread with half a fresh juicy tomato. If using, sprinkle over the chopped garlic and drizzle the olive oil over the top. Serve immediately.

spare ribs coated in paprika sauce

ingredients

serves 6

olive oil, for oiling
1.25 kg/2 lb 12 oz pork spare ribs
90 ml/3 fl oz dry Spanish sherry
5 tsp hot or sweet smoked
    Spanish paprika
2 garlic cloves, crushed
1 tbsp dried oregano
150 ml/5 fl oz water
salt

method

1 Oil a large roasting tin. If the butcher has not already done so, cut the sheets of spare ribs into individual ribs. If possible, cut each spare rib in half widthways. Put the spare ribs in the prepared tin, in a single layer, and roast in a preheated oven, 220°C/425°F/Gas Mark 7, for 20 minutes.

2 Meanwhile, make the sauce. Put the sherry, paprika, garlic, oregano, water and salt to taste in a jug and mix together well.

3 Reduce the oven temperature to 180°C/350°F/Gas Mark 4. Pour off the fat from the tin, then pour the sauce over the spare ribs and turn the spare ribs to coat on both sides. Roast for a further 45 minutes, until tender, basting the spare ribs with the sauce once halfway through the cooking time.

4 Pile the spare ribs into a warmed serving dish. Bring the sauce in the roasting tin to the boil on the hob, then reduce the heat and simmer until reduced by half. Pour the sauce over the spare ribs and serve hot.

pan-fried prawns

ingredients

serves 4

4 garlic cloves
20–24 large raw prawns
    in their shells
125 g/4½ oz butter
60 ml/2 fl oz olive oil
90 ml/3 fl oz brandy
salt and pepper
2 tbsp fresh chopped parsley,
    to garnish
lemon wedges, to serve

method

1 Using a sharp knife, peel and slice the garlic.

2 Wash the prawns and pat dry using kitchen paper.

3 Melt the butter with the oil in a large frying pan, add
   the garlic and prawns, and fry over a high heat, stirring,
   for 3–4 minutes, until the prawns are pink.

4 Sprinkle with brandy and season with salt and pepper
   to taste. Sprinkle with parsley and serve immediately,
   with lemon wedges for squeezing over the prawns.

variation

Instead of the brandy, use 1 tablespoon of soy sauce,
1 tablespoon of rice wine and 1 teaspoon of sugar.

sun-dried tomato & goat's cheese tarts

ingredients

serves 6

70 g/2½ oz sun-dried tomatoes
  in oil, drained and 2 tbsp oil
  reserved
1 courgette, thinly sliced
1 garlic clove, crushed
250 g/9 oz puff pastry,
  thawed if frozen
plain flour, for dusting
150 g/5½ oz soft goat's cheese
salt and pepper

method

1 Dampen a large baking sheet. Finely chop the sun-dried tomatoes and reserve. Heat 1 tablespoon of the reserved oil from the tomatoes in a large frying pan, add the courgette slices and cook over a medium heat, stirring occasionally, for 8–10 minutes, until golden brown on both sides. Add the garlic and cook, stirring, for 30 seconds. Remove from the heat and leave to cool completely while you prepare the pastry bases.

2 Thinly roll out the pastry on a lightly floured work surface. Using a plain, 9-cm/3½-inch cutter, cut out 12 rounds, re-rolling the trimmings as necessary. Transfer the rounds to the prepared baking sheet and prick 3–4 times with the tines of a fork. Divide the courgette mixture equally between the pastry rounds, add the tomatoes, leaving a 1-cm/½-inch border around the edge, and top each tart with a spoonful of goat's cheese. Drizzle over 1 tablespoon of the remaining oil from the tomatoes and season to taste with salt and pepper.

3 Bake the tarts in a preheated oven, 220°C/425°F/Gas Mark 7, for 10–15 minutes, until golden brown and well risen. Serve warm.

moroccan chicken kebabs

ingredients

serves 4

450 g/1 lb chicken breast fillets
3 tbsp olive oil, plus extra for oiling
juice of 1 lemon
2 garlic cloves, crushed
1½ tsp ground cumin
1 tsp ground coriander
1 tsp hot or sweet smoked
    Spanish paprika
¼ tsp ground cinnamon
½ tsp dried oregano
salt
chopped fresh flat-leaf parsley,
    to garnish

method

1 Cut the chicken into 2.5-cm/1-inch cubes and put in a large, shallow, non-metallic dish. Put all the remaining ingredients, except the parsley, in a bowl and whisk together. Pour the marinade over the chicken cubes and toss the meat in the marinade until well coated. Cover and leave to marinate in the refrigerator for 8 hours or overnight, turning the chicken 2–3 times if possible.

2 If using wooden skewers or cocktail sticks, soak the skewers in cold water for about 30 minutes, to help prevent them from burning and the food from sticking to them during cooking. If using metal skewers, lightly brush with oil. Preheat the grill, griddle or barbecue. Remove the chicken pieces from the marinade, reserving the remaining marinade, and thread an equal quantity onto each prepared skewer or cocktail stick, leaving a little space between each piece.

3 Brush the grill rack or griddle with a little oil, add the kebabs and cook, turning frequently and brushing with the reserved marinade halfway through cooking, for 15 minutes, or until browned on all sides, tender and cooked through. Serve hot, sprinkled with chopped parsley to garnish.

courgette fritters

ingredients

serves 6–8

450 g/1 lb baby courgettes
3 tbsp plain flour
1 tsp paprika
1 large egg
2 tbsp milk
sunflower oil, for pan-frying
coarse sea salt

pine kernel sauce

100 g/3½ oz pine kernels
1 garlic clove, peeled
3 tbsp extra virgin olive oil
1 tbsp lemon juice
3 tbsp water
1 tbsp chopped fresh flat-leaf
    parsley
salt and pepper

method

1 To make the pine kernel sauce, place the pine kernels
   and garlic in a food processor or blender and process
   to form a purée. Gradually add the olive oil, lemon
   juice and water to form a smooth sauce. Stir in the
   parsley and season to taste with salt and pepper.
   Transfer to a serving bowl and reserve until required.

2 To prepare the courgettes, cut them on the diagonal
   into thin slices about 5 mm/¼ inch thick. Place the
   flour and paprika in a polythene bag and mix together.
   Beat the egg and milk together in a large bowl.

3 Add the courgette slices to the flour mixture and toss
   well together until coated. Shake off the excess flour.
   Heat the sunflower oil in a large, heavy-based frying
   pan to a depth of about 1 cm/½ inch. Dip the slices,
   one at a time, into the egg mixture, then slip them into
   the hot oil. Fry the slices, in batches in a single layer
   so that they do not overcrowd the frying pan, for
   2 minutes, or until they are crisp and golden brown.

4 Using a slotted spoon, remove the courgette fritters
   from the frying pan and drain on kitchen paper.
   Continue until all the courgette slices have been fried.

5 Serve the courgette fritters piping hot, lightly sprinkled
   with sea salt, and accompanied by the pine kernel
   sauce for dipping.

olives with orange & lemon

ingredients

serves 4–6

2 tsp fennel seeds
2 tsp cumin seeds
225 g/8 oz green olives
225 g/8 oz black olives
2 tsp grated orange rind
2 tsp grated lemon rind
3 spring onions, finely chopped
pinch of ground cinnamon
60 ml/2 fl oz white wine vinegar
75 ml/2½ fl oz olive oil
2 tbsp orange juice
1 tbsp chopped fresh mint
1 tbsp chopped fresh parsley

method

1 Dry-fry the fennel seeds and cumin seeds in a small, heavy-based frying pan, shaking the pan frequently, until they begin to pop and give off their aroma. Remove the pan from the heat and set aside to cool completely.

2 Place the olives, orange and lemon rind, spring onions, cinnamon and toasted seeds in a bowl.

3 Whisk the vinegar, olive oil, orange juice, mint and parsley together in a bowl and pour over the olives. Toss well, then cover and allow the olives to chill in the refrigerator for 1–2 days before serving.

cracked marinated olives

ingredients

serves 8

450 g/1 lb can or jar unpitted large
    green olives, drained
4 garlic cloves, peeled
2 tsp coriander seeds
1 small lemon
4 sprigs of fresh thyme
4 feathery stalks of fennel
2 small fresh red chillies (optional)
extra virgin olive oil, to cover
pepper

method

1 To allow the flavours of the marinade to penetrate
   the olives, place the olives on a chopping board and,
   using a rolling pin, bash them lightly so that they
   crack slightly. Alternatively, use a sharp knife to cut a
   lengthways slit in each olive as far as the stone. Using
   the flat side of a broad knife, lightly crush each garlic
   clove. Using a pestle and mortar, crack the coriander
   seeds. Cut the lemon, with its rind, into small chunks.

2 Put the olives, garlic, coriander seeds, lemon chunks,
   thyme sprigs, fennel and chillies, if using, in a large
   bowl and toss together. Season with pepper to taste,
   but you should not need to add salt as preserved olives
   are usually salty enough. Pack the ingredients tightly
   into a glass jar with a lid. Pour in enough olive oil to
   cover the olives, then seal the jar tightly.

3 Allow the olives to stand at room temperature for
   24 hours, then marinate in the refrigerator for at least
   1 week but preferably 2 weeks before serving. From
   time to time, gently give the jar a shake to remix the
   ingredients. Return the olives to room temperature
   and remove from the oil to serve. Provide cocktail
   sticks for spearing the olives.

paprika-spiced almonds

ingredients
serves 4–6

1½ tbsp coarse sea salt
½ tsp smoked sweet Spanish
    paprika, or hot paprika,
    to taste
500 g/1 lb 2 oz blanched almonds
extra virgin olive oil, for drizzling

method

1 Place the sea salt and paprika in a mortar and grind with the pestle to a fine powder. Alternatively, use a mini spice blender (the amount is too small to process in a full-size processor).

2 Place the almonds on a baking sheet and roast in a preheated oven, 200°C/400°F/Gas Mark 6, for 8–10 minutes, stirring occasionally, until golden and giving off a toasted aroma. Watch after 7 minutes because they burn quickly. Pour into a heatproof bowl.

3 Drizzle over 1 tablespoon of olive oil and stir to ensure all the nuts are lightly and evenly coated. Add extra oil if necessary. Sprinkle with the salt and paprika mixture and stir again. Transfer to a small bowl and serve at room temperature.

variation
For a sweeter flavour, mix together 50 g/1¾ oz of sugar, 1 teaspoon of cinnamon, ½ teaspoon of cumin and less paprika to taste.

salted almonds

ingredients

serves 6–8

225 g/8 oz whole almonds, in their
skins or blanched (see method)
60 ml/2 fl oz olive oil
coarse sea salt
1 tsp paprika or ground cumin
(optional)

method

1 Fresh almonds in their skins are superior in taste but
blanched almonds are much more convenient. If the
almonds are not blanched, put them in a bowl, cover
with boiling water for 3–4 minutes, then plunge them
into cold water for 1 minute. Drain them well in a sieve,
then slide off the skins between your fingers. Dry the
almonds well on kitchen paper.

2 Put the olive oil in a roasting tin and swirl it round so
that it covers the bottom. Add the almonds and toss
them in the pan so that they are evenly coated in the
oil, then spread them out in a single layer.

3 Roast the almonds in a preheated oven, 180°C/350°F/
Gas Mark 4, for 20 minutes, or until they are light
golden brown, tossing several times during the
cooking. Drain the almonds on kitchen paper, then
transfer them to a serving bowl.

4 While the almonds are still warm, sprinkle with plenty
of sea salt and the paprika or cumin, if using, and toss
well together to coat. Serve the almonds warm or cold.

aubergine & pepper dip

ingredients

serves 6–8

2 large aubergines
2 red peppers
60 ml/2 fl oz olive oil
2 garlic cloves, roughly chopped
grated rind and juice of ½ lemon
1 tbsp chopped coriander,
    plus extra sprigs to garnish
½ –1 tsp paprika
salt and pepper
bread or toast, to serve

method

1 Prick the skins of the aubergines and peppers all over with a fork and brush with 1 tablespoon of the olive oil. Place on a baking sheet and bake in a preheated oven, 190°C/375°F/Gas Mark 5, for 45 minutes, or until the skins are beginning to turn black, the flesh of the aubergines is very soft and the peppers are deflated.

2 Place the cooked vegetables in a bowl and cover tightly with a clean, damp tea towel. Allow to stand for about 15 minutes, or until cool enough to handle, then cut the aubergines in half lengthways, carefully scoop out the flesh and discard the skin. Cut the aubergine flesh into large chunks. Remove and discard the stem, core and seeds from the peppers and cut the flesh into large pieces.

3 Heat the remaining olive oil in a frying pan. Add the vegetables and cook for 5 minutes. Add the garlic and cook for 30 seconds.

4 Drain the contents of the frying pan on kitchen paper, then transfer to a food processor. Add the lemon rind and juice, the chopped coriander, the paprika, and salt and pepper to taste, then process until a speckled purée is formed. Transfer the dip to a serving bowl. Serve warm or at room temperature. Garnish with coriander sprigs and accompany with bread or toast.

aubergine dip

ingredients

serves 6–8

75 ml/2½ fl oz olive oil
1 large aubergine,
    about 400 g/14 oz, sliced
2 spring onions, finely chopped
1 large garlic clove, crushed
2 tbsp finely chopped
    fresh parsley
salt and pepper
smoked sweet Spanish paprika,
    to garnish
crusty bread, to serve

method

1 Heat 4 tablespoons of the olive oil in a large frying pan over medium–high heat. Add the aubergine slices and cook on both sides until soft and beginning to brown. Remove from the frying pan and allow to cool completely. The slices will release the oil again as they cool.

2 Heat the remaining olive oil in the frying pan. Add the spring onions and garlic and cook for 3 minutes, or until the spring onions become soft. Remove from the heat and reserve with the aubergine slices to cool completely

3 Transfer all these ingredients to a food processor and process just until a coarse purée forms. Transfer to a serving bowl and stir in the parsley. Taste and adjust the seasoning, if necessary. Serve immediately, or cover and allow to chill in the refrigerator until 15 minutes before required. Sprinkle with paprika and serve with crusty bread.

potato wedges with roasted garlic dip

ingredients

serves 8

1.3 kg/3 lb potatoes,
    unpeeled and halved
2 tbsp olive oil
1 garlic clove, finely chopped
2 tsp salt

roasted garlic dip

2 garlic bulbs, separated
    into cloves
1 tbsp olive oil
75 ml/2½ fl oz soured cream
    or thick natural yogurt
60 ml/2 fl oz mayonnaise
salt
paprika, to taste

method

1 To make the roasted garlic dip, place the garlic cloves in an ovenproof dish, pour in the olive oil and toss to coat. Spread out in a single layer and roast in a preheated oven, 200°C/400°F/Gas Mark 6, for 25 minutes, or until tender. Remove from the oven and set aside until cool enough to handle.

2 Peel the garlic cloves, then place on a heavy chopping board and sprinkle with a little salt. Mash well with a fork until smooth. Scrape into a bowl and stir in the soured cream and mayonnaise. Season to taste with salt and paprika. Cover the bowl with clingfilm and allow to chill in the refrigerator until ready to serve.

3 To cook the potatoes, cut each potato half into 3 wedges and place in a large bowl. Add the olive oil, garlic and salt and toss well. Transfer the wedges to a roasting tin, then arrange in a single layer and roast in the preheated oven for 1–1¼ hours or until crisp and golden.

4 Remove the potatoes from the oven and transfer to serving bowls. Serve immediately, handing round the roasted garlic dip separately.

roasted asparagus with serrano ham

ingredients

serves 6

2 tbsp olive oil
6 slices Serrano ham
12 asparagus spears
pepper

aïoli

1 large egg yolk, at room
temperature
1 tbsp white wine vinegar
or lemon juice
2 large garlic cloves, peeled
75 ml/2½ fl oz extra virgin
olive oil
75 ml/2½ fl oz corn oil

method

1 To make the aïoli, blend the egg yolk, vinegar, garlic, and salt and pepper in a food processor. With the motor still running, very slowly add the olive oil, then the corn oil, drop by drop at first, then, when it starts to thicken, in a slow steady stream until the sauce is thick and smooth. Alternatively, mix in a bowl with a whisk.

2 Place half the olive oil in a roasting tin that will hold the asparagus spears in a single layer and swirl it around so that it covers the base. Cut each slice of Serrano ham in half lengthways.

3 Trim and discard the coarse woody ends of the asparagus spears, then wrap a slice of ham around the stem end of each spear. Place the wrapped spears in the prepared roasting tin and lightly brush with the remaining olive oil. Season the asparagus with the sea salt and pepper.

4 Roast the asparagus spears in a preheated oven, 200°C/ 400°F/Gas Mark 6, for 10 minutes, depending on the thickness of the asparagus, until tender but still firm. Do not overcook the asparagus spears as they should be firm enough to pick up. Serve the asparagus piping hot, accompanied by a bowl of aïoli for dipping.

chicken wings with tomato dressing

ingredients
serves 6

175 ml/6 fl oz olive oil
3 garlic cloves, finely chopped
1 tsp ground cumin
1 kg/2 lb 4 oz chicken wings
2 tomatoes, peeled, deseeded and diced
75 ml/2½ fl oz white wine vinegar
1 tbsp shredded fresh basil leaves

method

1 Mix 1 tablespoon of the oil, the garlic and the cumin together in a shallow dish. Cut off and discard the tips of the chicken wings and add the wings to the spice mixture, turning to coat. Cover with clingfilm and leave to marinate in a cool place for 15 minutes.

2 Heat 3 tablespoons of the remaining oil in a large, heavy-based frying pan. Add the chicken wings in batches and cook, turning frequently, until golden brown. Transfer to a roasting tin. Roast the chicken wings in a preheated oven at 180°C/350°F/Gas Mark 4, for 10–15 minutes, or until tender and the juices run clear when the point of a sharp knife is inserted into the thickest part of the meat.

3 Meanwhile, mix the remaining olive oil with the tomatoes, vinegar and basil in a bowl.

4 Using tongs, transfer the chicken wings to a non-metallic dish. Pour the dressing over them, turning to coat. Cover with clingfilm, leave to cool completely, then chill in the refrigerator for 4 hours. Remove from the refrigerator 30–60 minutes before serving, to return the chicken wings to room temperature.

garlic pan-fried bread & chorizo

ingredients

serves 6–8

200 g/7 oz chorizo sausage, outer
    casing removed
4 thick slices 2-day-old country
    bread
olive oil, for pan-frying
3 garlic cloves, finely chopped
2 tbsp chopped fresh
    flat-leaf parsley
paprika, to garnish

method

1 Cut the chorizo sausage into 1-cm/½-inch thick
  slices and cut the bread, with its crusts still on, into
  1-cm/½-inch cubes. Add enough olive oil to a large,
  heavy-based frying pan so that it generously covers
  the bottom. Heat the oil, add the garlic and cook for
  30 seconds–1 minute or until lightly browned.

2 Add the bread cubes to the frying pan and pan-fry,
  stirring all the time, until golden brown and crisp. Add
  the chorizo slices and pan-fry for 1–2 minutes, or until
  hot. Using a slotted spoon, remove the bread cubes
  and chorizo from the frying pan and drain well on
  kitchen paper.

3 Turn the pan-fried bread and chorizo into a warmed
  serving bowl, add the chopped parsley and toss
  together. Garnish the dish with a sprinkling of paprika
  and serve warm. Accompany with cocktail sticks so
  that a piece of sausage and a cube of bread can be
  speared together for eating.

sizzling chilli prawns

ingredients

serves 8

500 g/1 lb 2 oz raw king prawns,
    in their shells
1 small fresh red chilli
90 ml/6 fl oz olive oil
2 garlic cloves, finely chopped
pinch of paprika
salt
crusty bread, to serve

method

1 To prepare the prawns, pull off their heads. With your fingers, peel off their shells, leaving the tails intact. Using a sharp knife, make a shallow slit along the back of each prawn, then pull out the dark vein and discard. Rinse the prawns under cold water and dry well on kitchen paper.

2 Cut the chilli in half lengthways, remove the seeds and finely chop the flesh. It is important either to wear gloves while handling chillies or to wash your hands very thoroughly afterwards because their juices can cause irritation to sensitive skin, especially round the eyes, nose or mouth. Do not rub your eyes after touching the cut flesh of the chilli.

3 Heat the olive oil in a large, heavy-based frying pan or flameproof casserole until quite hot, then add the garlic and cook for 30 seconds. Add the prawns, chilli, paprika and a pinch of salt and cook for 2–3 minutes, stirring all the time, until the prawns turn pink and start to curl.

4 Serve the prawns in the cooking dish, still sizzling. Accompany with cocktail sticks to spear the prawns and chunks or slices of crusty bread to mop up the flavoured oil.

crab tartlets

ingredients

makes 24

1 tbsp olive oil
1 small onion, finely chopped
1 garlic clove, finely chopped
splash of dry white wine
2 eggs
150 ml/5 fl oz milk or single cream
175 g/6 oz canned crabmeat,
    drained
55 g/2 oz grated Manchego or
    Parmesan cheese
2 tbsp chopped fresh
    flat-leaf parsley
pinch of freshly grated nutmeg
salt and pepper
sprigs of fresh dill, to garnish

pastry

350 g/12 oz plain flour,
    plus extra for dusting
pinch of salt
175 g/6 oz butter
2 tbsp cold water

method

1 To prepare the crabmeat filling, heat the olive oil in a heavy-based frying pan, add the onion and cook for 5 minutes, or until softened but not browned. Add the garlic and cook for a further 30 seconds. Add a splash of wine and cook for 1–2 minutes, or until most of the wine has evaporated.

2 Lightly whisk the eggs in a large mixing bowl, then whisk in the milk or cream. Add the crabmeat, cheese, parsley and the onion mixture. Season with nutmeg and salt and pepper and mix well together.

3 To prepare the pastry, mix the flour and salt together in a large mixing bowl. Add the butter, cut into small pieces, and rub in until the mixture resembles fine breadcrumbs. Gradually stir in enough of the water to form a firm dough.

4 On a lightly floured work surface, thinly roll out the pastry. Using a plain, round 7-cm/2¾-inch cutter, cut out 24 circles. Use to line 24 x 4-cm/1½-inch tartlet tins. Carefully spoon the crabmeat mixture into the pastry cases, taking care not to overfill them. Bake in a preheated oven, 190°C/375°F/Gas Mark 5, for 25–30 minutes, or until golden brown and set. Serve the crab tartlets hot or cold, garnished with fresh dill sprigs.

spanish spinach & tomato pizzas

ingredients

makes 32

2 tbsp olive oil, plus extra for
    brushing and drizzling
1 onion, finely chopped
1 garlic clove, finely chopped
400 g/14 oz canned
    chopped tomatoes
125 g/4½ oz baby spinach leaves
2 tbsp pine kernels
salt and pepper

bread dough

60 ml/2 fl oz warm water
½ tsp easy-blend dried yeast
pinch of sugar
225 g/8 oz white bread flour,
    plus extra for dusting
½ tsp salt

method

1 To make the bread dough, place the water into a small
    bowl, sprinkle in the yeast and sugar and allow to stand
    in a warm place for 10–15 minutes, or until frothy.

2 Sift the flour and salt into a large bowl. Make a well in
    the centre, pour in the yeast, then stir together. Work
    the dough with your hands until it leaves the sides of
    the bowl clean. Turn out onto a lightly floured work
    surface and knead for 10 minutes, or until smooth and
    elastic. Put in a clean bowl, cover with a damp tea
    towel and stand in a warm place for 1 hour or until
    risen and doubled in size.

3 To make the topping, heat the olive oil in a large frying
    pan. Cook the onion until softened but not browned.
    Add the garlic and cook for 30 seconds. Stir in the
    tomatoes and cook until reduced to a thick sauce.
    Stir in the spinach leaves until wilted. Season to taste.

4 Turn the risen dough out and knead well for 2–3
    minutes. Roll out very thinly and, using a 6-cm/2½-inch
    plain round cutter, cut out 32 circles. Place on baking
    sheets brushed with olive oil. Cover each base with the
    spinach mixture. Sprinkle with pine kernels and drizzle
    over a little olive oil. Bake in a preheated oven, 200°C/
    400°F/Gas Mark 6, for 10–15 minutes, or until the edges
    of the dough are golden. Serve hot.

sautéed garlic mushrooms

ingredients

serves 6

450 g/1 lb button mushrooms
75 ml/2½ fl oz olive oil
2 garlic cloves, finely chopped
squeeze of lemon juice
3 tbsp chopped fresh
    flat-leaf parsley
salt and pepper
crusty bread, to serve

method

1 Wipe or brush clean the mushrooms, then trim off the stalks close to the caps. Cut any large mushrooms in half or into quarters. Heat the olive oil in a large, heavy-based frying pan, add the garlic and cook for 30 seconds–1 minute or until lightly browned. Add the mushrooms and sauté over high heat, stirring most of the time, until the mushrooms have absorbed all the oil in the frying pan.

2 Reduce the heat to low. When the juices have come out of the mushrooms, increase the heat again and sauté for 4–5 minutes, stirring most of the time, until the juices have almost evaporated. Add a squeeze of lemon juice and season to taste with salt and pepper. Stir in the chopped parsley and cook for a further minute.

3 Transfer the sautéed mushrooms to a warmed serving dish and serve piping hot or warm. Accompany with chunks or slices of crusty bread for mopping up the garlic cooking juices.

made with
vegetables

simmered summer vegetables

ingredients

serves 6–8

1 large aubergine
60 ml/2 fl oz olive oil
1 onion, thinly sliced
2 garlic cloves, finely chopped
2 courgettes, thinly sliced
1 red pepper, deseeded and
      thinly sliced
1 green pepper, deseeded
      and thinly sliced
8 tomatoes, peeled, deseeded,
      and chopped
salt and pepper
chopped fresh flat-leaf parsley,
      to garnish
slices of thick country bread,
      to serve (optional)

method

1 Cut the aubergine into 2.5-cm/1-inch cubes. Heat the oil in a large flameproof casserole, add the onion and cook over a medium heat, stirring occasionally, for 5 minutes, or until softened but not browned. Add the garlic to the casserole and cook, stirring, for 30 seconds until softened.

2 Increase the heat to medium–high, add the aubergine cubes and cook, stirring occasionally, for 10 minutes, or until softened and beginning to brown. Add the courgettes and peppers and cook, stirring occasionally, for 10 minutes, until softened. Add the tomatoes and season to taste with salt and pepper.

3 Bring the mixture to the boil, then reduce the heat, cover and simmer, stirring occasionally so that the vegetables do not stick to the base of the pan, for 15–20 minutes, until tender. If necessary, uncover, increase the heat and cook to evaporate any excess liquid, as the mixture should be thick.

4 Serve hot or cold, garnished with chopped parsley and accompanied by bread slices for scooping up the vegetables, if desired.

patatas bravas

ingredients

serves 6
2 tbsp olive oil
1 onion, finely chopped
2 garlic cloves, crushed
60 ml/2 fl oz white wine
    or dry Spanish sherry
400 g/14 oz canned chopped
    tomatoes
2 tsp white or red wine vinegar
1–2 tsp crushed dried chillies
2 tsp hot or sweet smoked
    Spanish paprika
1 kg/2 lb 4 oz potatoes
oil, for frying
salt

method

1 To make the sauce, heat the 2 tablespoons of oil in
   a saucepan, add the onion and cook over a medium
   heat, stirring occasionally, for 5 minutes, or until
   softened but not browned. Add the garlic and cook,
   stirring, for 30 seconds. Add the wine and bring to the
   boil. Add the tomatoes, vinegar, chillies and paprika,
   reduce the heat and simmer, uncovered, for 10–15
   minutes, until a thick sauce forms.

2 When the sauce is cooked, use a handheld blender to
   blend until smooth. Alternatively, transfer the sauce
   to a food processor and process until smooth. Return
   the sauce to the saucepan and set aside.

3 Do not peel the potatoes, but cut them into chunky
   pieces. Heat enough oil in a large frying pan to come
   about 2.5 cm/1 inch up the side of the pan. Add the
   potato pieces and cook over a medium–high heat,
   turning occasionally, for 10–15 minutes, until golden
   brown and tender. Remove with a slotted spoon, drain
   on kitchen paper and sprinkle with salt.

4 Meanwhile, gently reheat the sauce. Transfer the
   potatoes to a warmed serving dish and drizzle over the
   sauce. Serve hot, with wooden cocktail sticks to spear
   the potatoes.

fresh mint & bean pâté

ingredients

serves 12

800 g/1 lb 12 oz fresh broad beans
    in their pods, shelled to give
    about 350 g/12 oz
225 g/8 oz soft goat's cheese
1 garlic clove, crushed
2 spring onions, finely chopped
1 tbsp extra virgin olive oil, plus
    extra to serve
grated rind of lemon and
    2 tbsp juice
about 60 large fresh mint leaves,
    about 15 g/½ oz in total
salt and pepper
12 slices of French bread, to serve

method

1 Cook the broad beans in a saucepan of boiling water for 8–10 minutes, until tender. Drain well and leave to cool. When the beans are cool enough to handle, slip off their skins and put the beans in a food processor. This is a laborious task, but worth doing if you have the time. This quantity will take about 15 minutes to skin.

2 Add the goat's cheese, garlic, spring onions, oil, lemon rind and juice and mint leaves to the broad beans and process until well mixed. Season the pâté to taste with salt and pepper. Turn into a bowl, cover and chill in the refrigerator for at least 1 hour before serving.

3 Preheat the grill. To serve, toast the bread slices under a high grill until golden brown on both sides. Drizzle a little oil over the toasted bread slices, spread the pâté on top and serve immediately.

pickled stuffed peppers

ingredients

serves 6

200 g/7 oz Cuajada cheese, Queso del Tietar or other fresh goat's cheese
400 g/14 oz pickled peppers or pimientos del piquillo, drained
1 tbsp finely chopped fresh dill
salt and pepper

method

1 Cut the cheese into pieces about 1 cm/½ inch long. Slit the sides of the peppers and deseed, if you like. Stuff the peppers with the cheese.

2 Arrange the stuffed peppers on serving plates, sprinkle with the dill and season to taste with salt and pepper. Cover and chill in the refrigerator until ready to serve.

aubergine rolls

ingredients

serves 4

2 aubergines, thinly sliced
    lengthways
75 ml/2½ fl oz olive oil
1 garlic clove, crushed
60 ml/2 fl oz pesto
175 g/6 oz grated mozzarella
basil leaves, torn into pieces
salt and pepper
fresh basil leaves, to garnish

method

1 Sprinkle the aubergine slices liberally with salt and leave for 10–15 minutes to extract the bitter juices. Turn the slices over and repeat. Rinse well with cold water and drain on kitchen paper.

2 Heat the olive oil in a large frying pan and add the garlic. Fry the aubergine slices lightly on both sides, a few at a time. Drain them on kitchen paper.

3 Spread the pesto on to one side of the aubergine slices. Top with the grated mozzarella and sprinkle with the torn basil leaves. Season with a little salt and pepper. Roll up the slices and secure with wooden cocktail sticks.

4 Arrange the aubergine rolls in a greased ovenproof baking dish. Place in a preheated oven, 180°C/350°F/ Gas Mark 4, and bake for 8–10 minutes.

5 Transfer the aubergine rolls to a warmed serving plate. Scatter with fresh basil leaves and serve at once.

roasted pepper salad

ingredients

serves 8

3 red peppers
3 yellow peppers
75 ml/2½ fl oz extra virgin olive oil
2 tbsp dry sherry vinegar or lemon
    juice
2 garlic cloves, crushed
pinch of sugar
1 tbsp capers
8 small black olives
salt and pepper
2 tbsp chopped fresh marjoram,
    plus extra sprigs to garnish

method

1 Preheat the grill. Place the peppers on a wire rack or grill pan and cook under a high grill for 10 minutes, or until their skins have blackened and blistered, turning them frequently.

2 Remove the roasted peppers from the heat and either put them in a bowl and immediately cover tightly with a clean, damp tea towel or put them in a plastic bag. The steam helps to soften the skins and makes it easier to remove them. Set them aside for about 15 minutes, or until they are cool enough to handle.

3 Holding one pepper at a time over a clean bowl, use a sharp knife to make a small hole in the base and gently squeeze out the juices and reserve them. Still holding the pepper over the bowl, carefully peel off the blackened skin with your fingers or a knife and discard it. Cut the peppers in half and remove the stem, core and seeds, then cut each pepper into neat thin strips. Arrange the pepper strips on a serving dish.

4 Add the olive oil, sherry vinegar, garlic, sugar and salt and pepper to the reserved pepper juices. Whisk together until combined. Drizzle the dressing evenly over the salad. Sprinkle the capers, olives and chopped marjoram over the salad, garnish with marjoram sprigs and serve at room temperature.

roasted peppers with honey & almonds

ingredients

serves 6

8 red peppers, cut into quarters
    and deseeded
60 ml/2 fl oz olive oil
2 garlic cloves, thinly sliced
25 g/1 oz flaked almonds
2 tbsp clear honey
2 tbsp sherry vinegar
2 tbsp chopped fresh parsley
salt and pepper

method

1 Preheat the grill. Place the peppers, skin-side up, in a single layer on a baking sheet. Cook under a hot grill for 8–10 minutes, or until the skins have blistered and blackened. Using tongs, transfer the peppers to a plastic bag. Tie the top and set aside to cool.

2 When the peppers are cool enough to handle, peel off the skin with your fingers or a knife and discard it. Chop the pepper flesh into bite-size pieces and place in a bowl.

3 Heat the olive oil in a large, heavy-based frying pan. Add the garlic and cook over low heat, stirring frequently, for 4 minutes, or until golden. Stir in the almonds, honey and vinegar, then pour the mixture over the pepper pieces. Add the parsley and season to taste with salt and pepper, then toss well.

4 Allow to cool to room temperature, then transfer to serving dishes. The peppers may also be covered and stored in the refrigerator but should be returned to room temperature to serve.

stuffed peppers

ingredients

serves 6

90 ml/3 fl oz olive oil, plus a little
    extra for rubbing on peppers
2 onions, finely chopped
2 garlic cloves, crushed
140 g/5 oz Spanish
    short-grain rice
55 g/2 oz raisins
55 g/2 oz pine kernels
40 g/1½ oz finely chopped
    fresh parsley
1 tbsp tomato purée, dissolved in
    750 ml/1¼ pints hot water
6 red, green or yellow peppers
    (or a mix of colours)
salt and pepper

method

1 Heat the oil in a shallow, heavy-based flameproof
   casserole dish. Add the onions and cook for 3 minutes.
   Add the garlic and cook for a further 2 minutes, or until
   the onion is soft but not brown.

2 Stir in the rice, raisins and pine kernels until all are
   coated in the oil, then add half the parsley and salt
   and pepper to taste. Stir in the tomato purée mixture
   and bring to the boil. Reduce the heat and simmer,
   uncovered, shaking the casserole dish frequently,
   for 20 minutes, or until the rice is tender, the liquid
   is absorbed and small holes appear on the surface.
   Watch carefully because the raisins can catch and
   burn. Stir in the remaining parsley, then cool slightly.

3 While the rice is simmering, cut the top off each
   pepper and reserve. Remove the core and seeds from
   each pepper.

4 Divide the stuffing equally between the peppers. Use
   wooden cocktail sticks to secure the tops back in place.
   Lightly rub each pepper with olive oil and arrange in a
   single layer in an ovenproof dish. Bake in a preheated
   oven, 200°C/400°F/Gas Mark 6, for 30 minutes, or until
   the peppers are tender. Serve the peppers hot or cool
   to room temperature.

baby potatoes with aïoli

ingredients

serves 6–8

1 quantity aïoli (see page 36)
450 g/1 lb baby new potatoes
1 tbsp chopped fresh
     flat-leaf parsley
salt

method

1 Make the aïoli. For this recipe, the aïoli should be a little thinner so that it coats the potatoes when dipped. To ensure this, quickly blend in 1 tablespoon water so that it forms the consistency of a sauce. Set aside.

2 To prepare the potatoes, cut them in half or quarters to make bite-size pieces. If they are very small, you can leave them whole. Put the potatoes in a large saucepan of cold, salted water and bring to the boil. Lower the heat and simmer for 7 minutes, or until just tender. Drain well, then turn out into a large bowl.

3 Transfer the potatoes to a warmed serving dish, sprinkle over the parsley and salt and serve warm. Serve the aïoli separately, as a dipping sauce.

pan-fried potatoes with piquant paprika

ingredients

serves 6

3 tsp paprika
1 tsp ground cumin
$1/4 - 1/2$ tsp cayenne pepper
$1/2$ tsp salt
450 g/1 lb small old potatoes,
    peeled
corn oil, for pan-frying
sprigs of fresh flat-leaf parsley,
    to garnish

method

1 Put the paprika, cumin, cayenne pepper and salt in a small bowl and mix well together. Set aside.

2 Cut each potato into 8 thick wedges. Pour corn oil into a large, heavy-based frying pan to a depth of about 2.5 cm/1 inch. Heat the oil, then add the potato wedges, preferably in a single layer and cook gently for 10 minutes, or until golden brown all over, turning from time to time. Remove from the frying pan with a slotted spoon and drain on kitchen paper.

3 Transfer the potato wedges to a large bowl and, while they are still hot, sprinkle with the paprika mixture, then gently toss them together to coat.

4 Turn the potatoes into a large, warmed serving dish, several smaller ones or onto individual plates and serve hot, garnished with parsley sprigs.

warm potato salad

ingredients

serves 4–6

175 ml/6 fl oz olive oil
450 g/1 lb waxy potatoes,
   thinly sliced
60 ml/2 fl oz white wine vinegar
2 garlic cloves, finely chopped
salt and pepper

method

1 Heat 4 tablespoons of the olive oil in a large, heavy-based frying pan. Add the potato slices and season to taste with salt, then cook over low heat, shaking the frying pan occasionally, for 10 minutes. Turn the potatoes over and cook for a further 5 minutes, or until tender but not browned.

2 Meanwhile, pour the vinegar into a small saucepan. Add the garlic and season to taste with pepper. Bring to the boil, then stir in the remaining olive oil.

3 Transfer the potatoes to a bowl and pour over the dressing. Toss gently and set aside for 15 minutes. Using a slotted spoon, transfer the potatoes to individual serving dishes and serve warm.

green beans with pine kernels

ingredients

serves 8

2 tbsp olive oil
50 g/1¾ oz pine kernels
½–1 tsp paprika
450 g/1 lb green beans
1 shallot, finely chopped
1 garlic clove, finely chopped
juice of ½ lemon
salt and pepper

method

1 Heat the oil in a large, heavy-based frying pan, add the pine kernels and cook for about 1 minute, stirring all the time and shaking the frying pan, until light golden brown. Using a slotted spoon, remove the pine kernels from the frying pan, drain well on kitchen paper, then transfer to a bowl. Set aside the oil in the frying pan for later. Add the paprika to the pine kernels, stir together until coated and then set aside.

2 Trim the green beans and remove any strings if necessary. Put the beans in a saucepan, pour over boiling water, return to the boil and cook for 5 minutes, or until tender but still firm. Drain well in a sieve.

3 Reheat the oil in the frying pan, add the onion and cook for 5–10 minutes, or until softened and starting to brown. Add the garlic and cook for a further 30 seconds.

4 Add the beans to the frying pan and cook for 2–3 minutes, tossing together with the onion until heated through. Season the beans to taste with salt and pepper.

5 Turn the contents of the frying pan into a warmed serving dish, sprinkle over the lemon juice and toss together. Sprinkle over the golden pine kernels and serve hot.

mixed beans & peas

ingredients

serves 4–6

175 g/6 oz shelled fresh or frozen
   broad beans
115 g/4 oz fresh or frozen
   green beans
115 g/4 oz mangetout
1 shallot, finely chopped
6 fresh mint sprigs
60 ml/2 fl oz olive oil
1 tbsp sherry vinegar
1 garlic clove, finely chopped
salt and pepper

method

1 Bring a large saucepan of lightly salted water to the boil. Add the broad beans and reduce the heat, then cover and simmer for 7 minutes. Remove the beans with a slotted spoon, then plunge into cold water and drain. Remove and discard the outer skins.

2 Meanwhile, return the saucepan of salted water to the boil. Add the green beans and mangetout and return to the boil again. Drain and refresh under cold running water. Drain well.

3 Mix the broad beans, green beans, mangetout and shallot together in a bowl. Strip the leaves from the mint sprigs, then reserve half and add the remainder to the bean mixture. Finely chop the reserved mint.

4 Whisk the olive oil, vinegar, garlic and chopped mint together in a separate bowl and season to taste with salt and pepper. Pour the dressing over the bean mixture and toss lightly to coat. Cover with clingfilm and chill in the refrigerator until required.

garlic tomatoes

ingredients

serves 6

8 deep red tomatoes
3 fresh thyme sprigs, plus extra
    to garnish
12 garlic cloves, unpeeled
75 ml/2½ fl oz olive oil
salt and pepper

method

1 Cut the tomatoes in half lengthways and arrange,
   cut-side up, in a single layer in a large, ovenproof dish.
   Tuck the thyme sprigs and garlic cloves between them.

2 Drizzle the olive oil all over the tomatoes and season
   to taste with pepper. Bake in a preheated oven,
   220°C/425°F/Gas Mark 7, for 40–45 minutes, or until
   the tomatoes are softened and beginning to char
   slightly around the edges.

3 Remove and discard the thyme sprigs. Season the
   tomatoes to taste with salt and pepper. Garnish with
   the extra thyme sprigs and serve hot or warm.
   Squeeze the pulp from the garlic over the tomatoes
   at the table.

baked tomato nests

ingredients

serves 4

4 large ripe tomatoes
4 large eggs
60 ml/2 fl oz double cream
115 g/4 oz grated mature Mahon,
    Manchego or Parmesan cheese
salt and pepper

method

1 Cut a slice off the tops of the tomatoes and, using a teaspoon, carefully scoop out the pulp and seeds without piercing the shells. Turn the tomato shells upside down on kitchen paper and drain for 15 minutes. Season the insides of the shells with salt and pepper.

2 Place the tomatoes in an ovenproof dish just large enough to hold them in a single layer. Carefully break 1 egg into each tomato shell, then top with 1 tablespoon of cream and a quarter of the grated cheese.

3 Bake in a preheated oven, 180°C/350°F/Gas Mark 4, for 15–20 minutes, or until the eggs are just set. Serve hot.

artichoke hearts & asparagus

ingredients

serves 4–6

450 g/1 lb asparagus spears
400 g/14 oz canned artichoke
  hearts, drained and rinsed
2 tbsp freshly squeezed orange
  juice
½ tsp finely grated orange rind
2 tbsp walnut oil
1 tsp Dijon mustard
salt and pepper
salad leaves, to serve

method

1 Trim and discard the coarse, woody ends of the asparagus spears. Make sure all the stems are about the same length, then tie them together loosely with clean kitchen string. If you have an asparagus steamer, just place them directly in the basket.

2 Bring a tall saucepan of lightly salted water to the boil. Add the asparagus, making sure that the tips are protruding above the water, then reduce the heat and simmer for 10–15 minutes, or until tender. Test by piercing a stem just above the water level with the point of a sharp knife. Drain, then refresh under cold running water and drain again.

3 Cut the asparagus spears into 2.5-cm/1-inch pieces, keeping the tips intact. Cut the artichoke hearts into small wedges and combine with the asparagus in a bowl.

4 Whisk the orange juice, orange rind, walnut oil and mustard together in a bowl and seaon to taste with salt and pepper. If serving immediately, pour the dressing over the artichoke hearts and asparagus and toss lightly.

5 Arrange the salad leaves in individual serving dishes and top with the artichoke and asparagus mixture. Serve immediately.

stuffed mushrooms

ingredients

serves 6

175 g/6 oz butter
4 garlic cloves, finely chopped
6 large open mushrooms, stems
　　removed
55 g/2 oz fresh white breadcrumbs
1 tbsp chopped fresh thyme
1 egg, lightly beaten
salt and pepper

method

1 Cream the butter in a bowl until softened, then beat in the garlic. Divide two-thirds of the garlic butter between the mushroom caps and arrange them, cup-side up, on a baking sheet.

2 Melt the remaining garlic butter in a heavy-based or non-stick frying pan. Add the breadcrumbs and cook over low heat, stirring frequently, until golden. Remove from the heat and tip into a bowl. Stir in the thyme and season to taste with salt and pepper. Stir in the beaten egg until thoroughly combined.

3 Divide the breadcrumb mixture evenly between the mushroom caps and bake in a preheated oven, 180°C/350°F/Gas Mark 4, for 15 minutes, or until the stuffing is golden brown and the mushrooms are tender. Serve hot or warm.

marinated aubergines

ingredients

serves 4

2 aubergines, halved lengthways
60 ml/2 fl oz olive oil
2 garlic cloves, finely chopped
2 tbsp chopped fresh parsley
1 tbsp chopped fresh thyme
2 tbsp lemon juice
salt and pepper

method

1 Make 3 slashes in the flesh of the aubergine halves and place, cut-side down, in an ovenproof dish. Season to taste with salt and pepper, then pour over the olive oil and sprinkle with the garlic, parsley and thyme. Cover and marinate at room temperature for 2–3 hours.

2 Uncover the dish and roast the aubergines in a preheated oven, 180°C/350°F/Gas Mark 4, for 45 minutes. Remove the dish from the oven and turn the aubergines over. Baste with the cooking juices and sprinkle with the lemon juice. Return to the oven and cook for a further 15 minutes.

3 Transfer the aubergines to serving plates. Spoon over the cooking juices and serve hot or warm.

chargrilled leeks

ingredients

serves 4

8 baby leeks
2 tbsp olive oil, plus extra
    for brushing
2 tbsp white wine vinegar
2 tbsp snipped fresh chives
2 tbsp chopped fresh parsley
1 tsp Dijon mustard
salt and pepper
fresh parsley sprigs,
    to garnish

method

1 Trim the leeks and halve lengthways. Rinse thoroughly to remove any grit and pat dry with kitchen paper.

2 Heat a griddle pan and brush with olive oil. Add the leeks and cook over medium–high heat, turning occasionally, for 5 minutes. Transfer to a shallow dish.

3 Meanwhile, whisk the olive oil, vinegar, chives, parsley and mustard together in a bowl and season to taste with salt and pepper. Pour over the leeks, turning to coat. Cover with clingfilm and marinate at room temperature, turning occasionally, for 30 minutes.

4 Divide the leeks between individual serving plates, then garnish with parsley sprigs and serve.

orange & fennel salad

ingredients

serves 4

4 large, juicy oranges
1 large fennel bulb, very
  thinly sliced
1 mild white onion,
  finely sliced
2 tbsp extra virgin olive oil
12 plump black olives, pitted and
  thinly sliced
1 fresh red chilli, deseeded and
  very thinly sliced (optional)
finely chopped fresh parsley,
  to garnish
French bread, to serve

method

1 Finely grate the rind from the oranges into a bowl and reserve. Using a small, serrated knife, remove all the white pith from the oranges, working over a bowl to catch the juices. Cut the oranges horizontally into thin slices.

2 Toss the orange slices with the fennel and onion slices. Whisk the olive oil into the reserved orange juice, then spoon over the oranges. Sprinkle the olive slices over the top, add the chilli, if using, then sprinkle with the orange rind and parsley. Serve with slices of French bread.

tomato & olive salad

ingredients

serves 6

2 tbsp sherry or red wine vinegar
75 ml/2½ fl oz olive oil
1 garlic clove, finely chopped
1 tsp paprika
4 tomatoes, peeled and diced
12 anchovy-stuffed or
  pimiento-stuffed olives
½ cucumber, peeled and diced
2 shallots, finely chopped
1 tbsp pickled capers in brine,
  drained
2–3 chicory heads, separated
  into leaves
salt

method

1 To make the dressing, whisk the vinegar, olive oil, garlic and paprika together in a bowl. Season to taste with salt and reserve.

2 Place the tomatoes, olives, cucumber, shallots and capers in a separate bowl. Pour the dressing over and toss lightly.

3 Line six individual serving bowls with chicory leaves. Spoon an equal quantity of the salad into the centre of each and serve.

for meat lovers

calves' liver in almond saffron sauce

ingredients

serves 6

60 ml/2 fl oz olive oil
25 g/1 oz white bread
100 g/3½ oz blanched almonds
2 garlic cloves, crushed
pinch of saffron strands
150 ml/5 fl oz dry Spanish sherry
　　or white wine
300 ml/10 fl oz vegetable stock
450 g/1 lb calves' liver
plain flour, for dusting
salt and pepper
chopped fresh flat-leaf parsley,
　　to garnish
crusty bread, to serve

method

1 To make the sauce, heat 2 tablespoons of the oil in a large frying pan. Tear the bread into small pieces and add to the frying pan with the almonds. Cook over a low heat, stirring frequently, for 2 minutes, or until golden brown. Stir in the garlic and cook, stirring, for 30 seconds.

2 Add the saffron and sherry to the frying pan and season to taste with salt and pepper. Bring to the boil and continue to boil for 1–2 minutes. Remove from the heat and leave to cool slightly, then transfer the mixture to a food processor. Add the stock and process until smooth. Set aside.

3 Cut the liver into large bite-sized pieces. Dust lightly with flour and season generously with pepper. Heat the remaining oil in the frying pan, add the liver and cook over a medium heat, stirring constantly, for 2–3 minutes, until firm and lightly browned.

4 Pour the sauce into the frying pan and reheat gently for 1–2 minutes. Transfer to a warmed serving dish and garnish with chopped parsley. Serve hot, accompanied by chunks of crusty bread to mop up the sauce.

chorizo bread parcels

ingredients

serves 4

200 g/7 oz strong white flour,
plus extra for dusting
1½ tsp easy-blend dried yeast
½ tsp salt
¼ tsp caster sugar
125 ml/4 fl oz warm water
sunflower oil, for oiling
115 g/4 oz chorizo sausage,
outer casing removed, cut
into 16 equal-size chunks

method.

1 To make the bread dough, put the flour, yeast, salt and sugar in a large bowl and make a well in the centre. Pour the water into the well and gradually mix in the flour from the side. Mix together to form a soft dough.

2 Turn the dough onto a lightly floured work surface and knead for 10 minutes, or until smooth and elastic and no longer sticky. Shape the dough into a ball and put in a clean bowl. Cover with a clean, damp tea towel and leave in a warm place for 1 hour, or until the dough has risen and doubled in size.

3 Lightly oil a baking sheet. Turn out the risen dough onto a lightly floured work surface and knead lightly for 2–3 minutes to knock out the air.

4 Divide the dough into 16 equal-sized pieces. Shape each piece into a ball and roll out on a lightly floured work surface to a 12-cm/4½-inch round. Put a piece of chorizo on each round, gather the dough at the top, enclosing the chorizo, and pinch the edges to seal. Put each dough parcel, pinched-side down, on the prepared baking sheet.

5 Bake in a preheated oven, 200°C/400°F/Gas Mark 6, for 20 minutes, until pale golden brown. Turn the parcels over so that the pinched ends are facing up and arrange in a serving bowl or basket.

fried chorizo with herbs

ingredients

serves 6–8

700 g/1 lb 9 oz chorizo
    sausage
2 tbsp olive oil
2 garlic cloves, finely chopped
3 tbsp chopped mixed
    fresh herbs

method

1 Using a sharp knife, cut the chorizo into 5-mm/¼-inch thick slices. Heat a large, heavy-based frying pan. Add the chorizo slices, without any additional fat, and cook over medium heat, stirring frequently, for 5 minutes, or until crisp and browned.

2 Remove the chorizo slices with a spatula or slotted spoon and drain well on kitchen paper. Drain the fat from the frying pan and wipe out with kitchen paper.

3 Heat the olive oil in the frying pan over medium–low heat. Add the chorizo slices, garlic and herbs and cook, stirring occasionally, until heated through. Serve the chorizo in a warmed bowl immediately.

variation

Green and yellow peppers fried with the chorizo sausage make a colourful addition to this dish.

chickpeas & chorizo

ingredients

serves 4–6

250 g/9 oz chorizo sausage in
   1 piece, outer casing removed
60 ml/2 fl oz olive oil
1 onion, finely chopped
1 large garlic clove, crushed
400 g/14 oz canned chickpeas,
   drained and rinsed
6 pimientos del piquillo, drained,
   patted dry, and sliced
1 tbsp sherry vinegar,
   or to taste
salt and pepper
finely chopped fresh parsley,
   to garnish
crusty bread slices, to serve

method

1 Cut the chorizo into 1-cm/½-inch dice. Heat the oil in
   a heavy-based frying pan over medium heat, then add
   the onion and garlic. Cook, stirring occasionally, until
   the onion is softened but not browned. Stir in the
   chorizo and cook until heated through.

2 Tip the mixture into a bowl and stir in the chickpeas
   and pimientos. Splash with sherry vinegar and season
   to taste with salt and pepper. Serve hot or at room
   temperature, generously sprinkled with parsley, with
   plenty of crusty bread.

chorizo & mushroom kebabs

ingredients

makes 25

2 tbsp olive oil
25 pieces chorizo
    sausage, each about
    1-cm/½-inch square
    (about 100 g/3½ oz)
25 button mushrooms, wiped
    and stems removed
1 green pepper, grilled, peeled
    and cut into 25 squares

method

1 Heat the olive oil in a frying pan over medium heat. Add the chorizo pieces and cook them for about 20 seconds, stirring.

2 Add the mushrooms and continue cooking for a further 1–2 minutes, until the mushrooms begin to brown and absorb the fat in the pan.

3 Thread a pepper square, a piece of chorizo and a mushroom onto a wooden cocktail stick. Continue until all the ingredients are used. Serve the kebabs hot or at room temperature.

chorizo in red wine

ingredients

serves 6

200 g/7 oz chorizo sausage

200 ml/7 fl oz Spanish red wine

2 tbsp brandy (optional)

fresh flat-leaf parsley sprigs,
     to garnish

crusty bread, to serve

method

1 Using a fork, prick the chorizo in 3 or 4 places and pour wine over. Place the chorizo and wine in a large saucepan. Bring the wine to the boil, then reduce the heat and simmer gently, covered, for 15–20 minutes. Transfer the chorizo and wine to a bowl or dish, cover and leave the sausage marinate in the wine for 8 hours or overnight.

2 Remove the chorizo from the bowl or dish and reserve the wine. Remove the outer casing from the chorizo and cut the sausage into 5-mm/¼-inch slices. Place the slices in a large, heavy-based frying pan or flameproof serving dish.

3 If you are adding the brandy, pour it into a small saucepan and heat gently. Pour the brandy over the chorizo slices, then stand well back and set alight. When the flames have died down, shake the pan gently and add the reserved wine to the pan, then cook the chorizo over high heat until almost all of the wine has evaporated.

4 Serve the chorizo in red wine piping hot, in the dish in which it was cooked, sprinkled with parsley to garnish. Accompany with chunks or slices of bread to mop up the juices and provide wooden cocktail sticks to spear the pieces of chorizo.

broad beans with serrano ham

ingredients

serves 6–8

55 g/2 oz serrano or prosciutto
    ham, pancetta or rindless
    smoked lean bacon
115 g/4 oz chorizo sausage, outer
    casing removed
60 ml/2 fl oz olive oil
1 onion, finely chopped
2 garlic cloves, finely chopped
splash of dry white wine
450 g/1 lb frozen broad beans,
    thawed, or about 1.3 kg/3 lb
    fresh broad beans in their pods,
    shelled to give 450 g/1 lb
1 tbsp chopped fresh mint or dill,
    plus extra to garnish
pinch of sugar
salt and pepper

method

1 Using a sharp knife, cut the ham, pancetta or bacon
    into small strips. Cut the chorizo into 2-cm/³/₄-inch
    cubes. Heat the olive oil in a large, heavy-based frying
    pan or flameproof dish that has a lid. Add the onion
    and cook for 5 minutes, or until softened and starting
    to brown. If you are using pancetta or bacon, add it
    with the onion. Add the garlic and cook for 30 seconds.

2 Pour the wine into the pan, increase the heat and let it
    bubble to evaporate the alcohol, then lower the heat.
    Add the broad beans, ham, if using, and the chorizo
    and cook for 1–2 minutes, stirring all the time to coat
    in the oil.

3 Cover the frying pan and let the beans simmer very
    gently in the oil, stirring from time to time, for 10–15
    minutes, or until the beans are tender. It may be
    necessary to add a little water to the frying pan during
    cooking, so keep an eye on it and add a splash if the
    beans appear to become too dry. Stir in the mint or dill
    and sugar. Season the dish with salt and pepper but
    taste first as you may find that it does not need any salt.

4 Transfer the broad beans to a large, warmed serving
    dish, several smaller ones, or individual plates and serve
    piping hot, garnished with chopped mint or dill.

serrano ham with rocket

ingredients

serves 6

140 g/5 oz rocket, separated
　　into leaves
75 ml/2½ fl oz olive oil
1½ tbsp orange juice
280 g/10 oz thinly sliced
　　serrano ham
salt and pepper

method

1 Place the rocket in a bowl and pour in the olive oil
　and orange juice. Season to taste with salt and pepper
　and toss well.

2 Arrange the slices of ham on individual serving plates,
　folding it into attractive shapes. Divide the rocket
　between the plates and serve immediately.

variation

Try adding 200 g/7 oz of feta cheese and a handful of
black olives to this dish. Replace the orange juice with
a tablespoon of honey, if preferred.

tiny meatballs with tomato sauce

ingredients

makes 60

olive oil
1 red onion, very finely chopped
500 g/1 lb 2 oz fresh
    lamb mince
1 large egg, beaten
2 tsp freshly squeezed
    lemon juice
½ tsp ground cumin
pinch of cayenne pepper,
    to taste
2 tbsp very finely chopped
    fresh mint
salt and pepper

tomato sauce

60 ml/2 fl oz olive oil
10 large garlic cloves
140 g/5 oz spring onions, chopped
4 large red peppers, deseeded
    and chopped
1 kg/2 lb 4 oz ripe, fresh
    tomatoes, chopped
2 thin strips freshly pared
    orange rind
salt and pepper

method

1 To make the tomato sauce, heat the olive oil in a large casserole over medium heat. Add the garlic, spring onions and peppers and cook for 10 minutes, until the peppers are soft but not brown. Add the tomatoes and orange rind. Add salt and pepper to taste and bring to the boil. Reduce the heat and simmer, uncovered for 45 minutes, until the sauce thickens. Set aside until the meatballs are prepared.

2 Heat 1 tablespoon of olive oil in a frying pan over medium heat. Add the onion and cook for 5 minutes, stirring occasionally, until softened. Remove the pan from the heat and leave to cool until ready to handle. Add the onion to the lamb with the egg, lemon juice, cumin, cayenne, mint and salt and pepper in a large bowl. Squeeze all the ingredients together.

3 With wet hands, shape the mixture into about 60 x 2-cm/¾-inch balls. Place on a tray and chill in the refrigerator for at least 20 minutes.

4 When ready to cook, heat a small amount of olive oil in 1 or 2 large frying pans. Arrange the meatballs in a single layer and cook over medium heat for 5 minutes, or until brown on the outside but still pink inside.

5 Gently reheat the tomato sauce and serve with the meatballs for dipping.

mixed tapas platter with beef

ingredients

serves 8–10

200 g/7 oz small waxy potatoes, unpeeled

75 ml/2½ fl oz olive oil

2 sirloin steaks, about 225 g/8 oz each

1 fresh red chilli, deseeded and finely chopped (optional)

350 g/12 oz Queso del Montsec or other goat's cheese, sliced

175 g/6 oz mixed salad leaves

2 tbsp black olives

2 tbsp green olives

55 g/2 oz canned anchovies in oil, drained and halved lengthways

1 tbsp capers, drained and rinsed

salt and pepper

method

1 Cook the potatoes in a saucepan of lightly salted boiling water for 15–20 minutes, or until just tender. Drain and cool slightly.

2 Heat a heavy-based frying pan or griddle pan over high heat and brush with 1 tablespoon of the olive oil. Season the steaks to taste with pepper and add to the pan. Cook for 1–1½ minutes on each side, or until browned. Reduce the heat to medium and cook the steaks for 1½ minutes on each side. Remove and rest for 10–15 minutes.

3 Heat 2 tablespoons of the remaining oil in a frying pan. Add the chilli, if using, and the potatoes and cook, turning frequently, for 10 minutes, or until the potatoes are crisp and golden.

4 Thinly slice the steaks and arrange the slices alternately with the cheese slices along the sides of a serving platter. Mix the salad leaves, olives, anchovies and capers together, then arrange along the centre of the platter. Drizzle with the remaining oil, then top with the potatoes. Serve warm or at room temperature.

beef skewers
with orange & garlic

ingredients

serves 6–8

3 tbsp white wine

2 tbsp olive oil

3 garlic cloves, finely chopped

juice of 1 orange

450 g/1 lb rump steak, cubed

450 g/1 lb baby onions, halved

2 orange peppers, deseeded and
    cut into squares

225 g/8 oz cherry tomatoes,
    halved

salt and pepper

method

1 Mix the wine, olive oil, garlic and orange juice together
   in a shallow, non-metallic dish. Add the cubes of steak,
   season to taste with salt and pepper and toss to coat.
   Cover with clingfilm and marinate in the refrigerator
   for 2–8 hours.

2 Soak several wooden small skewers in cold water
   for 30 minutes before using. Preheat the grill to high.
   Drain the steak, reserving the marinade. Thread the
   steak, onions, peppers and tomatoes alternately onto
   the skewers.

3 Cook the skewers under the hot grill, turning and
   brushing frequently with the marinade, for 10 minutes,
   or until cooked through. Transfer to warmed serving
   plates and serve immediately.

citrus lamb skewers

ingredients

serves 8

2 garlic cloves, finely chopped
1 Spanish onion, finely chopped
2 tsp finely grated lemon rind
2 tbsp lemon juice
1 tsp fresh thyme leaves
1 tsp ground coriander
1 tsp ground cumin
2 tbsp red wine vinegar
125 ml/4 fl oz olive oil
1 kg/2 lb 4 oz lamb fillet, cut into
    2-cm/³/₄-inch pieces
orange or lemon slices,
    to garnish

method

1 Mix the garlic, onion, lemon rind, lemon juice, thyme, coriander, cumin, vinegar and olive oil together in a large, shallow, non-metallic dish, whisking the marinade well until combined.

2 Soak the wooden skewers in cold water before using. Thread the pieces of lamb onto the wooden skewers and add to the marinade, turning well to coat. Cover with clingfilm and marinate in the refrigerator for 2–8 hours, turning occasionally. Drain the skewers, reserving the marinade.

3 Preheat the grill to high. Cook the skewers under the hot grill, turning frequently and brushing with the marinade, for 10 minutes, or until tender and cooked to your liking. Serve immediately, garnished with orange slices.

miniature pork brochettes

ingredients

makes 12

450 g/1 lb lean boneless pork
3 tbsp olive oil, plus extra for
    oiling (optional)
grated rind and juice of
    1 large lemon
2 garlic cloves, crushed
2 tbsp chopped fresh
    flat-leaf parsley, plus extra
    to garnish
1 tbsp ras-el-hanout spice blend
salt and pepper

method

1 Cut the pork into pieces about 2 cm/³⁄₄ inch square and put in a large, shallow, non-metallic dish that will hold the pieces in a single layer.

2 To prepare the marinade, put the remaining ingredients in a bowl and mix well together. Pour the marinade over the pork and toss the meat in it until well coated. Cover the dish and marinate in the refrigerator for 8 hours or overnight, stirring the pork 2–3 times.

3 Soak the wooden skewers in cold water for 30 minutes before using. Preheat the grill, griddle pan, or barbecue. Thread 3 marinated pork pieces, leaving a little space between each piece, onto each skewer. Cook the brochettes for 10–15 minutes or until tender and lightly charred, turning several times and basting with the remaining marinade during cooking. Serve the pork brochettes piping hot, garnished with parsley.

chicken livers in sherry sauce

ingredients

serves 6

450 g/1 lb chicken livers
2 tbsp olive oil
1 small onion, finely chopped
2 garlic cloves, finely chopped
100 ml/3½ fl oz dry Spanish sherry
2 tbsp chopped fresh
   flat-leaf parsley
crusty bread or toast, to serve
salt and pepper

method

1 If necessary, trim the chicken livers, cutting away any ducts and gristle, then cut them into small, bite-size pieces.

2 Heat the olive oil in a large, heavy-based frying pan. Add the onion and cook for about 5 minutes, or until softened but not browned. Add the garlic to the pan and cook for a further 30 seconds.

3 Add the chicken livers to the pan and cook for 2–3 minutes, stirring all the time, until they are firm and have changed colour on the outside but are still pink and soft in the centre. Using a slotted spoon, lift the chicken livers from the pan, transfer them to a large, warmed serving dish and keep warm.

4 Add the sherry to the frying pan, increase the heat and let it bubble for 3–4 minutes to evaporate the alcohol and reduce slightly. At the same time, deglaze the frying pan by scraping and stirring all the bits on the bottom of the pan into the sauce with a wooden spoon. Season to taste with salt and pepper.

5 Pour the sherry sauce over the chicken livers and sprinkle over the parsley. Serve piping hot, with chunks or slices of crusty bread or toast to mop up the sherry sauce.

chicken rolls with olives

ingredients

serves 6–8

115 g/4 oz black olives
   in oil, drained
140 g/5 oz butter, softened
3 tbsp chopped fresh parsley
4 skinless, boneless
   chicken breasts
2 tbsp oil from the olive jar

method

1 Pit and chop the olives. Mix half the olives, the butter and the parsley together in a bowl.

2 Place the chicken breasts between two sheets of clingfilm and beat gently with a meat mallet or the side of a rolling pin.

3 Spread the olive and herb butter over one side of each flattened chicken breast and roll up. Secure with a wooden cocktail stick or tie with clean string if necessary to keep in place.

4 Place the chicken rolls in an ovenproof dish. Drizzle over the oil from the olive jar and bake in a preheated oven, 200°C/400°F/Gas Mark 6, for 45–55 minutes, or until tender and the juices run clear when the chicken is pierced with the point of a sharp knife.

5 Transfer the chicken rolls to a chopping board and discard the cocktail sticks or string. Using a sharp knife, cut into slices, then transfer to warmed serving plates. Scatter over the remaining olives and serve.

chicken in lemon & garlic

ingredients
serves 6–8

4 large skinless, boneless
    chicken breasts
75 ml/2½ fl oz olive oil
1 onion, finely chopped
6 garlic cloves, finely chopped
grated rind of 1 lemon, zest of
    1 lemon and juice of both
    lemons
3 tbsp chopped fresh flat-leaf
    parsley, plus extra to garnish
salt and pepper
lemon wedges and crusty bread,
    to serve

method

1 Using a sharp knife, slice the chicken breasts widthways into very thin slices. Heat the olive oil in a large, heavy-based frying pan, add the onion and cook for 5 minutes, or until softened but not browned. Add the garlic and cook for a further 30 seconds.

2 Add the sliced chicken to the frying pan and cook gently for 5–10 minutes, stirring from time to time, until all the ingredients are lightly browned and the chicken is tender.

3 Add the grated lemon rind and the lemon juice and let it bubble. At the same time, deglaze the frying pan by scraping and stirring all the bits on the bottom of the pan into the juices with a wooden spoon. Remove the pan from the heat, stir in the parsley and season to taste with salt and pepper.

4 Transfer, piping hot, to a warmed serving dish. Sprinkle with the lemon zest, garnish with the parsley and serve with lemon wedges for squeezing over the chicken, accompanied by chunks or slices of crusty bread for mopping up the juices.

for seafood fans

salt cod fritters with spinach

ingredients

serves 16

250 g/9 oz pre-soaked
      salt cod in 1 piece
2 lemon slices
2 fresh parsley sprigs
1 bay leaf
½ tbsp garlic-flavoured olive oil
85 g/3 oz fresh baby spinach,
      rinsed
¼ tsp smoked sweet, mild or hot
      Spanish paprika, to taste
Spanish olive oil, for frying
coarse sea salt (optional)
dipping sauce, to serve (optional)

batter

140 g/5 oz plain flour
1 tsp baking powder
¼ tsp salt
1 large egg, lightly beaten
about 150 ml/5 fl oz milk

method

1 To make the batter, sift the flour, baking powder and
   salt into a large bowl and make a well. Mix the egg with
   milk and pour into the well in the flour, stirring to make
   a smooth batter with a thick coating consistency. Leave
   to stand for at least 1 hour.

2 Transfer the salt cod to a large frying pan over a
   medium heat. Add the lemon slices, parsley sprigs, bay
   leaf and enough water to cover and bring to the boil.
   Reduce the heat and simmer for 30–45 minutes, until
   the fish is tender and flakes easily.

3 Meanwhile, heat the garlic oil in a small saucepan
   over a medium heat. Add the spinach and cook for
   3–4 minutes, until wilted. Drain and finely chop the
   spinach, then stir it into the batter with the paprika.

4 Remove the fish from the water and flake the flesh into
   pieces, removing all the skin and tiny bones. Stir the
   fish into the batter.

5 Heat 5 cm/2 inch of olive oil in a heavy-based frying
   pan to 180–190°C/350–375°F, or until a cube of bread
   browns in 30 seconds. Use a greased tablespoon to
   drop spoonfuls of the batter into the oil and fry for
   5 minutes, until golden brown. Transfer the fritters
   to kitchen paper to drain and sprinkle with sea salt,
   if using. Serve hot with a dipping sauce if liked.

salmon with red pepper sauce

ingredients

serves 6

2 red peppers
60 ml/2 fl oz olive oil
1 onion, roughly chopped
1 garlic clove, finely chopped
90 ml/3 fl oz/6 tbsp dry
    white wine
100 ml/3½ fl oz double cream
700 g/1 lb 9 oz salmon fillets,
    skinned and cut into cubes
salt and pepper
chopped fresh flat-leaf parsley,
    to garnish

method.

1 Brush the red peppers with 2 teaspoons of the oil and
    put in a roasting tin. Roast in a preheated oven, 200°C/
    400°F/Gas Mark 6, for 30 minutes, turn over and roast
    for a further 10 minutes, until the skins are blackened.

2 Heat 2 tablespoons of the remaining oil in a large frying
    pan, add the onion and cook for 5 minutes, or until
    softened. Add the garlic and cook for 30 seconds
    until softened. Add the wine and bring to the boil for
    1 minute. Remove from the heat and set aside.

3 When the peppers are cooked, transfer to a plastic bag,
    then tie the top and cool. Using a sharp knife or your
    fingers, carefully peel away the skin from the peppers.
    Halve, core and seed the peppers and put the flesh in
    a food processor. Add the onion mixture and cream to
    the peppers and process to a smooth purée. Season
    to taste with salt and pepper. Pour into a saucepan.

4 Heat the remaining oil in the frying pan, add the salmon
    cubes and cook, turning occasionally, for 8–10 minutes,
    until cooked through and golden brown on both sides.
    Meanwhile, gently heat the sauce in the saucepan.

5 Transfer the cooked salmon to a warmed serving dish,
    drizzle over some of the pepper sauce and serve the
    remaining sauce in a small serving bowl. Serve hot,
    garnished with chopped parsley.

saffron prawns with lemon mayonnaise

ingredients

serves 6–8

1.25 kg/2 lb 12 oz raw jumbo
    prawns
85 g/3 oz plain flour
125 ml/4 fl oz light beer
2 tbsp olive oil
pinch of saffron powder
2 egg whites
vegetable oil, for deep-frying

lemon mayonnaise

4 garlic cloves
2 egg yolks
1 tbsp lemon juice
1 tbsp finely grated lemon rind
300 ml/10 fl oz sunflower oil
salt and pepper

method

1 To make the mayonnaise, place the garlic cloves on a
chopping board and sprinkle with a little sea salt, and
finely chop. Transfer to a food processor or blender and
add the egg yolks, lemon juice and lemon rind. Process
briefly until just blended. Add the sunflower oil until
it is fully incorporated. Scrape the mayonnaise into a
serving bowl, season to taste with salt and pepper.
Cover and chill in the refrigerator until ready to serve.

2 Pull the heads off the prawns and peel, leaving the tails
intact. Cut along the length of the back of each prawn
and remove and discard the dark vein. Rinse under
cold running water and pat dry with kitchen paper.

3 Sift the flour into a bowl. Mix the beer, oil and saffron
together in a jug, then whisk into the flour. Cover and
leave for 30 minutes to rest. Whisk the egg whites in a
spotlessly clean, greasefree bowl until stiff. Gently fold
the egg whites into the flour mixture.

4 Heat the vegetable oil in a deep-fat fryer to 180–190°C/
350–375°F. Dip the prawns into the batter and shake
off any excess. Add the prawns to the oil and deep-fry
for 2–3 minutes, or until crisp. Remove and drain on
kitchen paper. Serve immediately with the mayonnaise.

mussels in a vinaigrette dressing

ingredients

serves 6

90 ml/3 fl oz extra virgin
olive oil

2 tbsp white wine vinegar

1 shallot, finely chopped

1 garlic clove, crushed

2 tbsp capers, chopped

1 fresh red chilli, deseeded and
finely chopped (optional)

1 kg/2 lb 4 oz live mussels,
in their shells

90 ml/3 fl oz dry white wine

3 tbsp chopped fresh
flat-leaf parsley

salt and pepper

crusty bread, to serve (optional)

method

1 To make the dressing, put the oil and vinegar in a bowl
and whisk together. Stir in the shallot, garlic, capers and
chilli, if using. Season to taste with salt and pepper.

2 Clean the mussels by scrubbing or scraping the shells
and pulling out any beards that are attached to them.
Discard any with broken shells or any that refuse to
close when tapped. Put the mussels in a colander and
rinse well under cold running water.

3 Put the mussels in a large saucepan and add the
wine. Bring to the boil, cover and cook over a high
heat, shaking the pan occasionally, for 3–4 minutes,
or until the mussels have opened. Drain the mussels,
discarding any that remain closed, and leave to cool.

4 When the mussels are cool enough to handle, discard
the empty half-shells and arrange the mussels, in their
other half-shells, in a large, shallow serving dish. Whisk
the dressing again and spoon over the mussels. Cover
and chill in the refrigerator for at least 1 hour.

5 To serve, sprinkle the parsley over the top and serve
with crusty bread to mop up the dressing, if desired.

clams in tomato & garlic sauce

ingredients

serves 6–8

2 hard-boiled eggs, cooled, shelled
    and halved lengthways
3 tbsp olive oil
1 Spanish onion, chopped
2 garlic cloves, finely chopped
700 g/1 lb 9 oz tomatoes, peeled
    and diced
40 g/1½ oz fresh white
    breadcrumbs
1 kg/2 lb 4 oz fresh clams
425 ml/15 fl oz dry white wine
2 tbsp chopped fresh parsley
salt and pepper
lemon wedges, to garnish

method

1 Scoop out the egg yolks using a teaspoon and rub
   through a fine sieve into a bowl. Chop the whites and
   reserve separately.

2 Heat the olive oil in a large, heavy-based frying pan.
   Add the onion and cook over a low heat, stirring
   occasionally, for 5 minutes, or until softened. Add the
   garlic and cook for a further 3 minutes, then add the
   tomatoes, breadcrumbs and egg yolks and season to
   taste with salt and pepper. Cook, stirring occasionally
   and mashing the mixture with a wooden spoon, for
   a further 10–15 minutes, or until thick and pulpy.

3 Meanwhile, scrub the clams under cold running water.
   Discard any with broken shells or any that do not close
   immediately when sharply tapped.

4 Place the clams in a large, heavy-based saucepan. Add
   the wine and bring to the boil. Cover and cook over a
   high heat, shaking the saucepan occasionally, for 3–5
   minutes, or until the clams have opened. Discard any
   that remain closed.

5 Using a slotted spoon, transfer the clams to warmed
   serving bowls. Strain the cooking liquid into the
   tomato sauce, stir well and spoon over the clams.
   Sprinkle with the chopped egg whites and parsley
   and serve immediately, garnished with lemon wedges.

batter-fried fish sticks

ingredients

serves 6

115 g/4 oz plain flour, plus
  extra for dusting
pinch of salt
1 egg, beaten
1 tbsp olive oil
150 ml/5 fl oz water
600 g/1 lb 5 oz firm-fleshed
  white fish fillet, such as
  monkfish or hake
sunflower or olive oil,
  for deep-frying
lemon wedges, to serve

method

1 To make the batter, put the flour and salt into a large bowl and make a well in the centre. Pour the egg and olive oil into the well, then gradually add the water, mixing in the flour from the side and beating constantly, until all the flour is incorporated and a smooth batter forms.

2 Cut the fish into sticks about 2 cm/¾ inch wide and 5 cm/2 inches long. Dust lightly with flour so that the batter sticks to them when they are dipped in it.

3 Heat enough sunflower or olive oil for deep-frying in a deep-fat fryer to 180–190°C/350–375°F. Spear a fish stick onto a cocktail stick, dip into the batter and then drop the fish and cocktail stick into the hot oil. Cook the fish sticks, in batches to avoid overcrowding, for 5 minutes, or until golden brown. Remove with a slotted spoon or draining basket and drain on kitchen paper. Keep hot in a warm oven while cooking the remaining fish sticks.

4 Serve the fish sticks hot, with lemon wedges for squeezing over.

monkfish, rosemary & bacon skewers

ingredients

serves 12

250 g/9 oz monkfish fillet
12 stalks of fresh rosemary
3 tbsp olive oil
juice of ½ small lemon
1 garlic clove, crushed
6 thick slices back bacon
salt and pepper
lemon wedges, to garnish
dipping sauce, to serve

method

1 Slice the monkfish fillet in half lengthways, then cut each fillet into 12 bite-size chunks to make a total of 24 pieces. Put the monkfish pieces in a large bowl.

2 To prepare the rosemary skewers, strip the leaves off the stalks and set them aside, leaving a few leaves at one end.

3 For the marinade, finely chop the reserved rosemary leaves and whisk together in a bowl with the olive oil, lemon juice, garlic and salt and pepper. Add the monkfish pieces and toss until coated in the marinade. Cover and marinate in the refrigerator for 1–2 hours.

4 Cut each bacon slice in half lengthways, then in half widthways, and roll up each piece. Thread 2 pieces of monkfish alternately with 2 bacon rolls onto each rosemary skewer.

5 Preheat the grill. Arrange the skewers on the grill pan so that the leaves of the rosemary skewers do not catch fire. Grill the skewers for 10 minutes, or until cooked, turning from time to time and basting with the marinade. Serve hot, garnished with lemon wedges and a bowl of dipping sauce.

traditional catalan salt cod salad

ingredients

serves 4–6

400 g/14 oz pre-soaked
salt cod in 1 piece

6 spring onions, thinly sliced
on the diagonal

90 ml/3 fl oz extra virgin olive oil

1 tbsp sherry vinegar

1 tbsp lemon juice

2 large red peppers, grilled, peeled,
deseeded and very finely diced

12 large black olives, pitted
and sliced

2 large, juicy tomatoes,
thinly sliced

pepper

2 tbsp very finely chopped fresh
parsley, to garnish

method

1 Pat the salt cod very dry with kitchen paper and remove the skin and bones. Use your fingers to tear into fine shreds. Place in a large, non-metallic bowl with the spring onions, olive oil, vinegar and lemon juice and toss together. Season with pepper, then cover and marinate in the refrigerator for 3 hours.

2 Stir in the peppers and olives. Taste and adjust the seasoning, if necessary, remembering that the cod and olives might be salty. Arrange the tomato slices on a large serving platter or individual serving plates and spoon the salad on top. Sprinkle with chopped parsley and serve.

catalan fish

ingredients

serves 4

4 globe artichokes, stems cut off,
   tough outer leaves removed
   and discarded, and points of
   the leaves trimmed with
   kitchen scissors
2 soles, filleted
½ lemon
225 ml/8 fl oz dry white wine
55 g/2 oz butter
2 tbsp plain flour
225 ml/8 fl oz milk
freshly grated nutmeg
bay leaf
115 g/4 oz sliced mushrooms
salt and pepper

method

1 Put the artichokes in a saucepan. Add water to cover and a pinch of salt. Bring to the boil, then simmer for 30 minutes, or until tender.

2 Season the fish fillets to taste and squeeze over the lemon. Cut each fillet into quarters lengthways, roll up and secure with a cocktail stick. Place in a shallow saucepan, then pour in the wine and poach gently, spooning over the wine occasionally, for 15 minutes.

3 Melt half the butter in a saucepan, then add the flour and cook, stirring, for 2 minutes. Stir in the milk. Bring to the boil, stirring constantly, until thick and smooth. Reduce the heat to very low, season to taste with salt and pepper. Add the nutmeg and the bay leaf.

4 Melt the remaining butter in a frying pan. Add the mushrooms and cook over medium heat, stirring occasionally, for 3 minutes. Remove from the heat.

5 Remove the artichokes from the pan with a slotted spoon and drain on kitchen paper. Remove and discard the hairy chokes and prickly leaves. Divide the mushrooms between the artichoke cavities and spoon in the sauce, discarding the bay leaf. Drain the fish fillets with a slotted spoon and remove and discard the cocktail sticks. Place two fillets in each of the artichoke cavities and serve.

sardines with lemon & chilli

ingredients

serves 4

450 g/1 lb fresh sardines, scaled, cleaned and heads removed
60 ml/2 fl oz lemon juice
1 garlic clove, finely chopped
1 tbsp finely chopped fresh dill
1 tsp finely chopped fresh red chilli
60 ml/2 fl oz olive oil
salt and pepper

method

1 Place the sardines, skin-side up, on a chopping board and press along the length of the spines with your thumbs. Turn them over and remove and discard the bones.

2 Place the fillets, skin-side down, in a shallow, non-metallic dish and sprinkle with the lemon juice. Cover with clingfilm and stand in a cool place for 30 minutes.

3 Drain off any excess lemon juice. Sprinkle the garlic, dill and chilli over the fish and season to taste with salt and pepper. Drizzle over the olive oil, then cover with clingfilm and chill in the refrigerator for 12 hours before serving.

sardines marinated in sherry vinegar

ingredients

serves 6

175 ml/6 fl oz olive oil

12 small fresh sardines, cleaned and filleted, and heads and tails removed if wished

60 ml/2 fl oz sherry vinegar

2 carrots, cut into julienne strips

1 onion, thinly sliced

1 garlic clove, crushed

1 bay leaf

3 tbsp chopped fresh flat-leaf parsley

salt and pepper

few sprigs of fresh dill, to garnish

lemon wedges, to serve

method

1 Heat 4 tablespoons of the olive oil in a large, heavy-based frying pan. Add the sardines and cook for 10 minutes, or until browned on both sides. Using a spatula, very carefully remove the sardines from the pan and transfer to a large, shallow, non-metallic dish that will hold the sardines in a single layer.

2 Gently heat the remaining olive oil and the sherry vinegar in a large saucepan, add the carrot strips, onion, garlic and bay leaf and simmer gently for 5 minutes, or until softened. Season the vegetables to taste with salt and pepper. Allow the mixture to cool slightly, then pour the marinade over the sardines.

3 Cover the dish and allow the sardines to cool completely before transferring to the refrigerator. Marinate for about 8 hours or overnight, spooning the marinade over the sardines occasionally. Return the sardines to room temperature before serving. Sprinkle with parsley, garnish with dill sprigs and serve with lemon wedges.

pickled mackerel

ingredients

serves 6

8 fresh mackerel fillets
300 ml/10 fl oz extra virgin
    olive oil
2 large red onions, thinly sliced
2 carrots, sliced
2 bay leaves
2 garlic cloves, thinly sliced
2 dried red chillies
1 fennel bulb, halved and
    thinly sliced
300 ml/10 fl oz sherry vinegar
1½ tbsp coriander seeds
salt and pepper
toasted crusty bread, to serve

method

1 Preheat the grill. Place the mackerel fillets, skin-side up, on a grill rack and brush with oil. Cook under a hot grill, about 10 cm/4 inches from the heat source, for 4–6 minutes, or until the skins become brown and crispy and the flesh flakes easily. Reserve until required.

2 Heat the remaining oil in a large frying pan. Add the onions and cook for 5 minutes, or until softened but not browned. Add the remaining ingredients and simmer for 10 minutes, or until the carrots are tender.

3 Flake the mackerel flesh into large pieces, removing the skin and tiny bones. Place the mackerel pieces in a preserving jar and pour over the onion, carrot and fennel mixture. (The jar should accommodate everything packed in quite tightly with the minimum air gap at the top once the vegetable mixture has been poured in.) Cool the jar completely, then cover tightly and chill in the refrigerator for at least 24 hours and up to 5 days. Serve the pieces of mackerel on toasted slices of crusty bread with a little of the oil drizzled over.

4 Alternatively, serve the mackerel and its pickled vegetables as a first-course salad.

tuna, egg & potato salad

ingredients

serves 4

350 g/12 oz new potatoes,
    unpeeled
1 hard-boiled egg, cooled
    and shelled
3 tbsp olive oil
1½ tbsp white wine vinegar
115 g/4 oz canned tuna in oil,
    drained and flaked
2 shallots, finely chopped
1 tomato, peeled and diced
2 tbsp chopped fresh parsley
salt and pepper

method

1 Cook the potatoes in a saucepan of lightly salted boiling water for 10 minutes, then remove from the heat, cover and leave to stand for 15–20 minutes, or until tender.

2 Meanwhile, slice the egg, then cut each slice in half. Whisk the olive oil and vinegar together in a bowl and season to taste with salt and pepper. Spoon a little of the vinaigrette into a serving dish to coat the base.

3 Drain the potatoes, then peel and thinly slice. Place half the slices over the base of the dish and season to taste with salt, then top with half the tuna, half the egg slices and half the shallots. Pour over half the remaining dressing. Make a second layer with the remaining potato slices, tuna, egg and shallots, then pour over the remaining dressing.

4 Finally, top the salad with the tomato and parsley. Cover with clingfilm and stand in a cool place for 1–2 hours before serving.

tuna rolls

ingredients

serves 4

3 red peppers
125 ml/4 fl oz olive oil
2 tbsp lemon juice
75 ml/2½ fl oz red wine vinegar
2 garlic cloves, finely chopped
1 tsp paprika
1 tsp dried chilli flakes
2 tsp sugar
2 tbsp salted capers
200 g/7 oz canned tuna in oil,
    drained and flaked

method

1 Preheat the grill. Place the peppers on a baking sheet. Cook under the preheated grill for 10 minutes, turning frequently, or until the skin is blackened all over. Using tongs, transfer the peppers to a plastic bag, then tie the top and cool.

2 Meanwhile, whisk the olive oil, lemon juice, vinegar, garlic, paprika, chilli flakes and sugar together in a small bowl.

3 When the peppers are cool enough to handle, peel off the skins, deseed then cut the flesh into thirds lengthways. Place the pepper pieces in a non-metallic dish and pour over the dressing, turning to coat. Stand in a cool place for 30 minutes.

4 Rub the salt off the capers and mix with the tuna. Drain the pepper pieces, reserving the dressing. Divide the tuna mixture between the pepper pieces and roll up. Secure with wooden cocktail sticks. Place the tuna rolls on a serving platter, then spoon over the dressing and serve at room temperature.

anchovy & spinach empanadillas

ingredients

serves 6–8

500 g/1 lb 2 oz fresh
 spinach leaves
2 tbsp olive oil, plus extra
 for brushing
2 garlic cloves, finely chopped
8 canned anchovy fillets in oil,
 drained and chopped
2 tbsp raisins, soaked in hot water
 for 10 minutes
40 g/1½ oz pine kernels
450 g/1 lb puff pastry,
 thawed if frozen
plain flour, for dusting
1 egg, lightly beaten
salt and pepper

method

1 Trim and discard any tough stems from the spinach and
 finely chop the leaves.

2 Heat the olive oil in a large saucepan. Add the chopped
 spinach, then cover and cook over low heat, gently
 shaking the pan occasionally, for 3 minutes. Stir in the
 garlic and anchovies and cook, uncovered, for a further
 1 minute. Remove from the heat.

3 Drain the raisins and chop, then stir them into the
 spinach mixture with the pine kernels and salt and
 pepper to taste. Allow to cool.

4 Roll out the pastry on a lightly floured work surface
 to a circle about 3 mm/⅛ inch thick. Stamp out
 circles using a 7.5-cm/3-inch biscuit cutter. Re-roll
 the trimmings and stamp out more circles.

5 Place 1–2 heaped teaspoonfuls of the spinach filling
 onto each pastry round. Brush the edges with water
 and fold over to make half moons. Press together well
 to seal. Lightly brush 1–2 baking sheets with olive oil.
 Place the empanadillas on baking trays and brush with
 beaten egg to glaze, then bake in a preheated oven,
 180°C/350°F/Gas Mark 4, for 15 minutes, or until golden
 brown. Serve warm.

calamares

ingredients

serves 6

450 g/1 lb prepared squid
plain flour, for coating
corn oil, for deep-frying
salt
lemon wedges, to garnish
aïoli sauce, to serve (see page 36)

method

1 Make 1 quantity of aïoli sauce.

2 Slice the squid into 1-cm/½-inch rings and halve the tentacles, if large. Rinse and dry well on kitchen paper so that they do not spit during cooking. Dust the squid rings with flour so that they are lightly coated. Do not season the flour, as this will toughen the squid.

3 Heat the oil in a deep-fryer to 180–190°C/350–375°F. Carefully add the squid rings, in batches so that the temperature of the oil does not drop, and deep-fry for 2–3 minutes, or until golden brown and crisp all over, turning several times. Do not overcook as the squid will become tough and rubbery rather than moist and tender.

4 Using a slotted spoon, remove the deep-fried squid from the deep-fryer and drain well on kitchen paper. Transfer to a warm oven while you deep-fry the remaining squid rings.

5 Sprinkle the deep-fried squid with salt and serve piping hot, garnished with lemon wedges for squeezing over them. Accompany with a bowl of dipping sauce to dip the pieces in.

giant garlic prawns

ingredients

serves 4

125 ml/4 fl oz olive oil
4 garlic cloves, finely chopped
2 hot fresh red chillies, deseeded
    and finely chopped
450 g/1 lb cooked king prawns
2 tbsp chopped fresh
    flat-leaf parsley
salt and pepper
lemon wedges, to garnish
crusty bread, to serve

method

1 Heat the olive oil in a preheated wok or large, heavy-based frying pan over low heat. Add the garlic and chillies and cook, stirring occasionally, for 1–2 minutes, or until softened but not coloured.

2 Add the prawns and stir-fry for 2–3 minutes, or until heated through and coated in the garlic mixture.

3 Turn off the heat and add the chopped parsley, stirring well to mix. Season to taste with salt and pepper.

4 Divide the prawns and garlic-flavoured oil between warmed serving dishes and garnish with lemon wedges. Serve with crusty bread.

lime-drizzled prawns

ingredients

serves 6

4 limes
12 raw king prawns,
    in their shells
3 tbsp olive oil
2 garlic cloves, finely chopped
splash of fino sherry
3 tbsp chopped fresh
    flat-leaf parsley
salt and pepper

method

1 Grate the rind and squeeze the juice from 2 of the limes. Cut the remaining 2 limes into wedges and set aside for later.

2 To prepare the prawns, remove the head and legs, leaving the shells and tails intact. Using a sharp knife, make a shallow slit along the back of each prawn, then pull out the dark vein and discard. Rinse the prawns under cold water and dry on kitchen paper.

3 Heat the olive oil in a large, heavy-based frying pan, then add the garlic and cook for 30 seconds. Add the prawns and cook for 5 minutes, stirring from time to time, or until they turn pink and start to curl. Mix in the lime rind and juice and a splash of sherry to moisten, then stir well together.

4 Transfer the cooked prawns to a serving dish, season to taste with salt and pepper, and sprinkle with the parsley. Serve piping hot, accompanied by the reserved lime wedges for squeezing over the prawns.

garlic prawns with lemon & parsley

ingredients

serves 6

60 raw jumbo prawns,
   thawed if using frozen
150 ml/5 fl oz olive oil
6 garlic cloves, thinly sliced
3 dried hot red chillies (optional)
90 ml/3 fl oz freshly squeezed
   lemon juice
60 g/2¼ oz very finely chopped
   fresh parsley
French bread, to serve

method

1 Peel and devein the prawns and remove the heads, leaving the tails on. Rinse and pat the prawns dry.

2 Heat the olive oil in a large, deep sauté pan or frying pan. Add the garlic and chillies, if using, and stir constantly until they begin to sizzle. Add the prawns and cook until they turn pink and begin to curl.

3 Use a slotted spoon to transfer the prawns to warm earthenware bowls. Sprinkle each bowl with lemon juice and parsley. Serve with plenty of bread to mop up the juices.

baked scallops

ingredients

serves 4

700 g/1 lb 9 oz scallops, shelled
    and chopped
2 onions, finely chopped
2 garlic cloves, finely chopped
3 tbsp chopped fresh parsley
pinch of freshly grated nutmeg
pinch of ground cloves
2 tbsp fresh white breadcrumbs
2 tbsp olive oil
salt and pepper

method

1 Mix the scallops, onions, garlic, 2 tablespoons of the parsley, the nutmeg and cloves together in a bowl and season to taste with salt and pepper.

2 Divide the mixture between 4 scrubbed scallop shells or heatproof dishes. Sprinkle the breadcrumbs and remaining parsley on top and drizzle with the olive oil.

3 Bake the scallops in a preheated oven, 200°C/400°F/ Gas Mark 6, for 15–20 minutes, or until lightly golden and piping hot. Serve immediately.

seared scallops

ingredients

serves 4–6

60 ml/2 fl oz olive oil
3 tbsp orange juice
2 tsp hazelnut oil
24 scallops, shelled
salad leaves (optional)
175 g/6 oz Cabrales or other
    blue cheese, crumbled
2 tbsp chopped fresh dill
salt and pepper

method

1 Whisk 3 tablespoons of the olive oil, the orange juice and the hazelnut oil together in a jug and season to taste with salt and pepper.

2 Heat the remaining olive oil in a large, heavy-based frying pan. Add the scallops and cook over high heat for 1 minute on each side, or until golden.

3 Transfer the scallops to a bed of salad leaves or individual plates. Scatter over the cheese and dill, then drizzle with the dressing and serve warm.

clams with broad beans

ingredients

serves 4–6

4 canned anchovy fillets
   in oil, drained

1 tsp salted capers

3 tbsp olive oil

1 tbsp sherry vinegar

1 tsp Dijon mustard

500 g/1 lb 2 oz fresh clams

about 175 ml/6 fl oz water

500 g/1 lb 2 oz broad beans,
   shelled if fresh

2 tbsp chopped mixed fresh
   herbs, such as parsley,
   chives and mint

salt and pepper

method

1 Place the anchovies in a small bowl, then add water to cover and soak for 5 minutes. Drain well, then pat dry with kitchen paper and place in a mortar. Brush the salt off the capers, then add to the mortar and pound to a paste with a pestle.

2 Whisk the olive oil, vinegar and mustard together in a separate bowl, then whisk in the anchovy paste and season to taste with pepper. Cover with clingfilm and stand at room temperature until required.

3 Scrub the clams under cold running water. Discard any with broken shells or any that do not close immediately when sharply tapped. Place the clams in a large saucepan and add the water. Cover and bring to the boil over high heat. Cook, shaking the pan occasionally, for 3–5 minutes, or until the clams have opened. Discard any that remain closed.

4 Bring a large saucepan of lightly salted water to the boil. Add the broad beans, then return to the boil and blanch for 5 minutes. Drain, then refresh under cold running water and drain again. Remove and discard the outer skins and place the broad beans in a bowl.

5 Drain the clams and remove them from their shells. Add to the beans and sprinkle with the herbs. Add the anchovy vinaigrette and toss lightly. Serve warm.

of eggs
& cheese

asparagus scrambled eggs

ingredients

serves 6

450 g/1 lb asparagus, trimmed
    and roughly chopped
2 tbsp olive oil
1 onion, finely chopped
1 garlic clove, finely chopped
6 eggs
1 tbsp water
6 small slices country bread
salt and pepper

method

1 Steam the asparagus pieces for 8 minutes, or cook in
    a large saucepan of boiling salted water for 4 minutes,
    until just tender, depending on their thickness. Drain
    well, if necessary.

2 Meanwhile, heat the oil in a large frying pan, add
    the onion and cook over a medium heat, stirring
    occasionally, for 5 minutes, or until softened but
    not browned. Add the garlic and cook, stirring, for
    30 seconds until softened.

3 Stir the asparagus into the frying pan and cook,
    stirring occasionally, for 3–4 minutes. Meanwhile,
    break the eggs into a bowl, add the water and beat
    together. Season to taste with salt and pepper.

4 Add the beaten eggs to the asparagus mixture and
    cook, stirring constantly, for 2 minutes, or until the
    eggs have just set. Remove from the heat.

5 Preheat the grill. Toast the bread slices under the
    hot grill until golden brown on both sides. Pile the
    scrambled eggs on top of the toast and serve
    immediately.

stuffed eggs with anchovies & cheese

ingredients

serves 8

8 eggs
50 g/1¾ oz canned anchovy fillets
   in olive oil, drained
55 g/2 oz grated Manchego cheese
60 ml/2 fl oz extra virgin
   olive oil
1 tbsp freshly squeezed lemon
   juice
1 garlic clove, crushed
4 stoned green Spanish olives,
   halved
salt and pepper
4 stoned black Spanish olives,
   halved
hot or sweet smoked Spanish
   paprika, for dusting

method.

1 Put the eggs in a saucepan, cover with cold water and slowly bring to the boil. Reduce the heat and simmer gently for 10 minutes. Immediately drain the eggs and rinse under cold running water to cool. Gently tap the eggs to crack the shells and leave until cold.

2 When the eggs are cold, crack the shells all over and remove them. Using a stainless steel knife, halve the eggs, carefully remove the egg yolks and put the yolks in a food processor.

3 Add the anchovy fillets, Manchego cheese, oil, lemon juice and garlic to the egg yolks and process to a purée. Season to taste with salt and pepper.

4 Using a teaspoon, spoon the mixture into the egg white halves. Alternatively, using a piping bag fitted with a 1-cm/½-inch plain nozzle, pipe the mixture into the egg white halves. Arrange the stuffed eggs on a serving dish, cover and chill in the refrigerator until ready to serve.

5 To serve, put an olive half on the top of each stuffed egg and dust with paprika.

chorizo & broad bean tortilla

ingredients

serves 9

225 g/8 oz frozen baby
    broad beans
6 eggs
100 g/3½ oz chorizo sausage,
    outer casing removed,
    chopped
3 tbsp olive oil
1 onion, chopped
salt and pepper

method

1 Cook the broad beans in a saucepan of boiling water
    for 4 minutes. Drain well and leave to cool. Meanwhile,
    lightly beat the eggs in a large bowl. Add the chorizo
    sausage and season to taste with salt and pepper.

2 When the beans are cool enough to handle, slip off
    their skins. This is a laborious task, but worth doing
    if you have the time. This quantity will take about
    15 minutes to skin.

3 Heat the oil in a large frying pan, add the onion and
    cook over a medium heat, stirring occasionally, for
    5 minutes, or until softened but not browned. Add the
    broad beans and cook, stirring, for 1 minute. Pour the
    egg mixture into the frying pan and cook gently for
    2–3 minutes, until the underside is just set and lightly
    browned. Use a spatula to loosen the tortilla away
    from the side and base of the frying pan to allow the
    uncooked egg to run underneath and prevent the
    tortilla from sticking to the base.

4 Cover the tortilla with a large, upside-down plate and
    invert the tortilla onto it. Slide the tortilla back into
    the frying pan, cooked-side up, and cook for a further
    2–3 minutes, until the underside is lightly browned.

5 Slide the tortilla onto a warmed serving dish. Serve
    warm, cut into small cubes.

spinach & mushroom tortilla

ingredients

serves 8

2 tbsp olive oil
3 shallots, finely chopped
350 g/12 oz sliced mushrooms
280 g/10 oz fresh spinach leaves,
    coarse stalks removed
55 g/2 oz toasted flaked almonds
5 eggs
2 tbsp chopped fresh parsley
2 tbsp cold water
85 g/3 oz grated, mature Mahon,
    Manchego or Parmesan cheese
salt and pepper

method

1 Heat the olive oil in a frying pan that can safely be placed under the grill. Add the shallots and cook over a low heat, stirring occasionally, for 5 minutes, or until softened. Add the mushrooms and cook, stirring frequently, for a further 4 minutes. Add the spinach, increase the heat to medium and cook, stirring frequently, for 3–4 minutes, or until wilted. Reduce the heat, season to taste with salt and pepper and stir in the flaked almonds.

2 Beat the eggs with the parsley, water and salt and pepper to taste in a bowl. Pour the mixture into the pan and cook for 5–8 minutes, or until the underside is set. Lift the edge of the tortilla occasionally to allow the uncooked egg to run underneath.

3 Preheat the grill. Sprinkle the grated cheese over the tortilla and cook under the grill for 3 minutes, or until the top is set and the cheese has melted. Serve, lukewarm or cold, cut into thin wedges.

tortilla española

ingredients

serves 4

350 ml/12 fl oz olive oil
450 g/1 lb waxy potatoes, cubed
2 onions, chopped
4 large eggs
salt and pepper
olives (optional)
sprigs of fresh flat-leaf parsley,
    to garnish

method

1 Heat the olive oil in a large, heavy-based frying pan. Add the potato cubes and onions, then lower the heat and cook, stirring frequently, for 20 minutes, or until tender but not browned. Drain the potatoes and onions well, setting aside the oil.

2 Beat the eggs lightly in a large bowl and season well with salt and pepper. Stir in the potatoes and onions.

3 Wipe out the frying pan with kitchen paper and heat 2 tablespoons of the reserved olive oil. When hot, add the egg and potato mixture, lower the heat and cook for 3–5 minutes, or until the underside is just set. Use a spatula to submerge the potatoes in the egg and loosen the tortilla from the bottom of the frying pan to stop it sticking.

4 Cover the tortilla with a plate and hold the plate in place with the other hand. Drain off the oil in the frying pan, then quickly invert the tortilla onto the plate. Return the frying pan to the heat and add a little more oil if necessary. Slide the tortilla, cooked side uppermost, back into the frying pan and cook for a further 3–5 minutes, or until set underneath.

5 Slide the tortilla onto a serving plate and let stand for about 15 minutes. Serve warm or cold in slices, with olives if wished, garnished with parsley sprigs.

spicy stuffed eggs

ingredients

serves 6

6 hard-boiled eggs, cooled
    and shelled
3 tbsp grated Manchego or
    Cheddar cheese
1–2 tbsp mayonnaise
2 tbsp snipped fresh chives
1 fresh red chilli, deseeded
    and finely chopped
salt and pepper
salad leaves, to serve

method

1 Cut the eggs in half lengthways and, using a teaspoon, carefully scoop out the yolks into a fine sieve, reserving the egg white halves. Rub the yolks through the sieve into a bowl and add the grated cheese, mayonnaise, chives, chilli and salt and pepper. Spoon the filling into the egg white halves.

2 Arrange a bed of salad leaves on individual serving plates and top with the eggs. Cover and chill in the refrigerator until ready to serve.

flamenco eggs

ingredients

serves 4

60 ml/2 fl oz olive oil
1 onion, thinly sliced
2 garlic cloves, finely chopped
2 small red peppers, deseeded
    and chopped
4 tomatoes, peeled, deseeded
    and chopped
1 tbsp chopped fresh parsley
200 g/7 oz canned sweetcorn,
    drained
4 eggs
salt and cayenne pepper

method

1 Heat the olive oil in a large, heavy-based frying pan. Add the onion and garlic and cook over low heat, stirring occasionally, for 5 minutes, or until softened. Add the red peppers and cook, stirring occasionally, for a further 10 minutes. Stir in the tomatoes and parsley, season to taste with salt and cayenne pepper and cook for a further 5 minutes. Stir in the sweetcorn and remove the pan from the heat.

2 Divide the mixture between 4 individual ovenproof dishes. Make a hollow in the surface of each using the back of a spoon. Break an egg into each hollow.

3 Bake in a preheated oven, 180°C/350°F/Gas Mark 4, for 15–25 minutes, or until the eggs have set. Serve hot.

basque scrambled eggs

ingredients

serves 4–6

45–60 ml/1½–2 fl oz olive oil
1 large onion, finely chopped
1 large red pepper, deseeded
    and chopped
1 large green pepper, deseeded
    and chopped
2 large tomatoes, peeled, deseeded
    and chopped
55 g/2 oz chorizo sausage, thinly
    sliced, outer casing removed,
    if preferred
35 g/1¼ oz butter
10 large eggs, lightly beaten
salt and pepper
4–6 thick slices country-style
    bread, toasted, to serve

method

1 Heat 2 tablespoons of olive oil in a large, heavy-based
    frying pan over medium heat. Add the onion and
    peppers and cook for 5 minutes, or until the vegetables
    are softened but not browned. Add the tomatoes and
    heat through. Transfer to a heatproof plate and keep
    warm in a preheated low oven.

2 Add another tablespoon of oil to the frying pan. Add
    the chorizo and cook for 30 seconds, just to warm
    through and flavour the oil. Add the chorizo to the
    reserved vegetables.

3 Add a little extra olive oil, if necessary, to the frying pan,
    to bring it back to 2 tablespoons. Add the butter and
    let it melt. Season the eggs with salt and pepper, then
    add to the frying pan and scramble until cooked to the
    desired degree of firmness. Return the vegetables and
    chorizo to the pan and stir through. Serve immediately
    on hot toast.

chorizo & quail's eggs

ingredients

serves 12

12 slices French bread, sliced on
the diagonal, about
5 mm/¼ inch thick
40 g/1½ oz cured, ready-to-eat
chorizo, cut into 12 thin slices
olive oil
12 quail's eggs
mild paprika
salt and pepper
fresh flat-leaf parsley, to garnish

method

1 Preheat the grill to high. Arrange the slices of bread on a baking sheet and grill until golden on both sides.

2 Cut or fold the thin chorizo slices to fit on the toasts, then reserve.

3 Heat a thin layer of olive oil in a large frying pan over medium heat. Break the eggs into the frying pan and cook, spooning the fat over the yolks, until the whites are set and the yolks are cooked to your liking.

4 Remove the fried eggs from the frying pan and drain on kitchen paper. Immediately transfer to the chorizo-topped toasts and dust with paprika. Season to taste with salt and pepper, then garnish with parsley and serve immediately.

deep-fried manchego cheese

ingredients

serves 6-8

200 g/7 oz Manchego cheese
3 tbsp plain flour
1 egg
1 tsp water
85 g/3 oz fresh white or brown
    breadcrumbs
corn oil, for deep-frying
salt and pepper

method

1 Slice the cheese into triangular shapes about 2 cm/
  $^3/_4$ inch thick. Put the flour in a plastic bag and season
  with salt and pepper to taste. Break the egg into a
  shallow dish and beat together with the water. Spread
  out the breadcrumbs on a plate.

2 Toss the cheese pieces in the flour so that they are
  evenly coated, then dip the cheese in the egg mixture.
  Finally, dip the cheese in the breadcrumbs so that the
  pieces are coated on all sides.

3 Just before serving, heat about 2.5 cm/1 inch of the
  corn oil in a large, heavy-based frying pan or heat the
  oil in a deep-fryer to 180–190°C/350–375°F or until a
  cube of bread browns in 30 seconds. Add the cheese
  pieces, in batches of about 4 or 5 pieces so that the
  temperature of the oil does not drop, and deep-fry
  for 1–2 minutes, turning once, until the cheese is just
  starting to melt and they are golden brown on all sides.
  Do make sure that the oil is hot enough, otherwise the
  coating on the cheese will take too long to become
  crisp and the cheese inside may ooze out.

4 Using a slotted spoon, remove the cheese from the
  frying pan or deep-fryer and drain well on kitchen
  paper. Serve hot.

cheese puffs with fiery tomato salsa

ingredients

serves 8

70 g/2½ oz plain flour
60 ml/2 fl oz olive oil
150 ml/5 fl oz water
2 eggs, beaten
55 g/2 oz finely grated Manchego,
    Parmesan, Cheddar, Gouda
    or Gruyère cheese
½ tsp paprika
corn oil, for deep-frying
salt and pepper

tomato salsa
2 tbsp olive oil
1 small onion, finely chopped
1 garlic clove, crushed
splash of dry white wine
400 g/14 oz canned chopped
    tomatoes
1 tbsp tomato purée
¼–½ tsp dried red pepper flakes
dash of Tabasco sauce
pinch of sugar
salt and pepper

method

1 To make the salsa, heat the olive oil in a saucepan, add the onion and cook until softened but not browned. Add the garlic and cook for 30 seconds. Add the wine and let it bubble, then add the remaining salsa ingredients and simmer, uncovered, until a thick sauce is formed. Set aside.

2 Meanwhile, prepare the cheese puffs. Sift the flour onto a plate. Put the olive oil and water in a pan and slowly bring to the boil. As soon as the water boils, remove the pan from the heat and quickly tip in the flour. Using a wooden spoon, beat the mixture well until it is smooth and leaves the sides of the pan.

3 Cool for 1–2 minutes, then gradually add the eggs, beating hard after each addition and keeping the mixture stiff. Add the cheese and paprika, season to taste with salt and pepper and mix well together.

4 To cook the cheese puffs, heat the corn oil in a deep-fryer to 180–190°C/350–375°F. Drop teaspoonfuls of the prepared mixture into the hot oil and deep-fry for 2–3 minutes, turning once, or until golden and crispy. They should rise to the surface and puff up. Drain well. Serve the puffs piping hot, with the tomato salsa.

figs with blue cheese

ingredients

serves 6

12 ripe figs
350 g/12 oz Spanish blue cheese,
   such as Picos, crumbled
extra virgin olive oil, to serve

caramelized almonds

100 g/3½ oz caster sugar
115 g/4 oz whole almonds
butter, for greasing

method

1 First make the caramelized almonds. Place the sugar in
   a saucepan over medium heat and stir until the sugar
   melts and turns golden brown and bubbles. Do not stir
   once the mixture begins to bubble. Remove the pan
   from the heat, then add the almonds one at a time
   and quickly turn with a fork until coated. If the caramel
   hardens, return the pan to the heat. Transfer each
   almond to a lightly greased baking sheet once it is
   coated. Set aside until firm and completely cooled.

2 To serve, slice the figs in half and arrange 4 halves on
   individual serving plates. Roughly chop the almonds by
   hand. Place a mound of blue cheese on each plate and
   sprinkle with chopped almonds. Drizzle the figs very
   lightly with the olive oil.

cheese & shallots
with herb dressing

ingredients

serves 6

1 tsp sesame seeds

¼ tsp cumin seeds

4 tomatoes, deseeded and diced

75 ml/2½ fl oz olive oil

60 ml/2 fl oz lemon juice

2 tsp chopped fresh thyme

1 tbsp chopped fresh mint

4 shallots, finely chopped

500 g/1 lb 2 oz Idiazabal or other
     sheep's milk cheese, diced

salt and pepper

method

1 Dry-fry the sesame and cumin seeds in a small,
   heavy-based frying pan, shaking the pan frequently,
   until they begin to pop and give off their aroma.
   Remove from the heat and set aside to cool.

2 Place the tomatoes in a bowl. To make the dressing,
   whisk the olive oil and lemon juice together in a
   separate bowl. Season to taste with salt and pepper,
   then add the thyme, mint and shallots and mix well.

3 Place the cheese in another bowl. Pour half the
   dressing over the tomatoes and toss lightly. Cover
   with clingfilm and chill in the refrigerator for 1 hour.
   Pour the remaining dressing over the cheese, then
   cover and chill for 1 hour.

4 To serve, divide the cheese mixture between six
   serving plates and sprinkle with half the toasted seeds.
   Top with the tomato mixture and sprinkle with the
   remaining toasted seeds.

roasted peppers with fiery cheese

ingredients

serves 6

1 red pepper, halved and deseeded
1 orange pepper, halved and deseeded
1 yellow pepper, halved and deseeded
115 g/4 oz Afuega'l Pitu cheese or other hot spiced cheese, diced
1 tbsp clear honey
1 tbsp sherry vinegar
salt and pepper

method

1 Preheat the grill. Place the peppers, skin-side up, in a single layer on a baking sheet. Cook under the hot grill for 8–10 minutes, or until the skins have blistered and blackened. Using tongs, transfer the peppers to a plastic bag. Tie the top and set aside to cool.

2 When the peppers are cool enough to handle, peel off the skin with your fingers or a knife and discard it. Place on a serving plate and sprinkle over the cheese.

3 Whisk the honey and vinegar together in a bowl and season to taste with salt and pepper. Pour the dressing over the peppers, then cover and chill in the refrigerator until required.

burgos with sherry vinegar

ingredients

serves 4

400 g/14 oz Burgos cheese
1–2 tbsp clear honey
3 tbsp sherry vinegar
carrot sticks
chilled sherry, to serve

method

1 Place the cheese in a bowl and beat until smooth, then beat in 1 tablespoon of the honey and 1 ½ tablespoons of the vinegar.

2 Taste and adjust the sweetness to taste by adding more honey or more vinegar as required.

3 Divide between four small serving bowls, then cover and chill in the refrigerator until required. Serve with carrot sticks and chilled sherry.

cheese & olive empanadillas

ingredients

makes 26

85 g/3 oz firm or soft cheese

85 g/3 oz pitted green olives

55 g/2 oz sundried tomatoes
in oil, drained

50 g/1¾ oz canned anchovies,
drained

2 tbsp sundried tomato purée

plain flour, for dusting

500 g/1 lb 2 oz ready-made puff
pastry, thawed if frozen

beaten egg, to glaze

pepper

fresh flat-leaf parsley sprigs,
to garnish

method

1 Cut the cheese into small dice measuring about 5 mm/¼ inch. Chop the olives, sundried tomatoes and anchovies into pieces about the same size as the cheese. Put all the chopped ingredients in a bowl, season with pepper to taste and gently mix together. Stir in the sundried tomato purée.

2 On a lightly floured work surface, thinly roll out the puff pastry. Using a plain, round 8-cm/3¼-inch cutter, cut into 18 circles. Gently pile the trimmings together, roll out again, then cut out an additional 8 circles. Using a teaspoon, put a little of the prepared filling in the centre of each circle.

3 Dampen the edges of the pastry with a little water, then bring up the sides to cover the filling completely and pinch the edges together with your fingers to seal them. With the tip of a sharp knife, make a small slit in the top of each pastry. You can store the pastries in the refrigerator until you are ready to bake them.

4 Place the pastries onto dampened baking sheets and brush each with a little beaten egg to glaze. Bake in a preheated oven, 200°C/400°F/Gas Mark 6, for 10–15 minutes, or until golden brown, crisp and well risen. Serve the empanadillas piping hot, warm or cold, garnished with parsley sprigs.

index